George Mason's America: The State Sovereignty Alternative to Madison's Centralized American Ruling Class Aristocracy.

Laurie Thomas Vass

Copyright © 2023 The Great American Business & Economics Press. GABBYPress.com

First edition. All rights reserved under Title 17, U.S. Code, International and Pan-American copyright Conventions.

No part of this work may be reproduced or transmitted in any form or by any means, electronic or mechanical, including photocopying, scanning, recording or duplication by any information storage or retrieval system without prior written permission from the author(s) and publisher(s), except for the inclusion of brief quotations with attribution in a review or report. Requests for reproductions or related information should be addressed to the author c/o Great American Business & Economics Press, 620 Kingfisher Lane SW, Sunset Beach, N. C. 28468.

Printed in the United States of America. April 2023

Table of Contents

Preface	5
Chapter 1. Solving The Mystery of Mason's Obscurity In American History.	15
Chapter 2. Mason's Egalitarian Principles of Individual Rights and His Concept of the State Sovereignty Constitutional Framework of Liberty.	50
Chapter 3. Mason's Lifetime Crusade Against the Corruption and Tyranny Inherent in the British Mixed Social Class Conflict Model.	71
Chapter 4. Shays' Rebellion and Madison's War Against State-Issued Paper Money.	98
Chapter 5. James Buchanan' Individual Rights Constitutional Rules For Maximum Social Prosperity.	146
Chapter 6. The Evolutionary Entrepreneurial Capitalist Economy of Joseph Schumpeter.	186
Chapter 7. George Mason's America: The Emergence of A Stable Entrepreneurial Capitalist Society.	226
Bibliography	249

Preface: George Mason's America: The State Sovereignty Alternative to Madison's Centralized American Ruling Class Aristocracy.

Our book is about George Mason's vision of American society, as an alternative to Madison's constitutional design.

Our intent is to argue that Mason's egalitarian concept of political rights, had it been implemented in 1787, would have been a better path for liberty for American middle and working class citizens, than Madison's framework, that ended with the agencies of government in the hands of an unelected deep state ruling class tyranny.

The difference between Mason's vision and Madison's constitution is the difference between a decentralized state sovereignty framework, which would have promoted the economic interests of common citizens, and Madison's centralized ruling class aristocracy, which permanently elevated the financial interests of wealthy American citizens over the interests of common citizens.

Our main economic argument in favor of Mason's vision of America is that it would have led to the emergence of a stable middle class social order, which would have eliminated the ruling class' ability to manipulate money supply and interest rates, through the unelected power of the various central national banks.

We agree with the economic theory of Adam Smith that the working of the free competitive market leads society to maximum social prosperity, given the proviso that promotion of the sovereign national economic interest is the end goal of market exchange.

The 38 delegates who signed the constitution on September 17, 1787, created rules that benefitted themselves, as the nation's wealthy social class, to the detriment of the financial interests of common citizens.

After the Constitution was signed, the ruling class implemented banking and financial rules that permanently elevated their financial interests over the financial interests of common citizens.

Our argument is not simply that the individual wealthy citizens had common financial interests in forming the constitution. (Beard, Charles A., An Economic Interpretation of the Constitution of the United States. The Macmillan Company. 1914.).

The key factor to understand in the creation of Madison's rules is that the aristocracy in America had a unified, coherent social class awareness of the type of rules that would benefit their social class.

Madison's logic of the extended republic, in Federalist #10 was based upon the false premise that the common citizens in England already had formed a social class consciousness, and that the American common citizens would likely form their own awareness of their class interests.

Madison was afraid that, if the American common citizens developed a coherent class awareness, like the English class consciousness, the as-yet-uncreated imaginary American common class consciousness would compete with the natural aristocracy.

Madison's rules, as he explained in Federalist #10, would extend the republic in such a way as to eliminate the possibility that middle class citizens would ever form a social class awareness to disrupt the status quo financial privileges of the ruling class faction.

Our premise in arguing for a new constitution to replace Madison's constitution is that his representative republic ended in November of 2020, with massive election fraud.

Madison's constitution is too broken to be repaired, through amendments. (Feldman, Noah, The Broken Constitution: Lincoln, Slavery, and the Refounding of America, Farrar, Straus & Giroux, 2021.)

George Mason objected to Madison's consolidated all powerful central government, and insisted that Madison's constitution violated the spirit of liberty of the American Revolution.

William Hyland writes,

"Mason's struggle with Madison and Washington over the powers in the Constitution was a fight over the meaning of political liberty, and the last real battle of the Revolution…Mason was convinced that the fundamental principles of the Revolution stood in jeopardy." (William G. Hyland, Jr., George Mason: The Founding Father Who Gave Us The Bill of Rights, Regnery History, 2019.).

Our book is divided into three parts.

In the first part, we describe Mason's individualist concept of society and contrast Mason's concept with the evolution of Madison's centralized deep state bureaucracy.

In the second part of the book, we rely on the constitutional theory of James Buchanan to build out the details of what Mason's philosophy of individual freedom, would look like in a decentralized state sovereignty constitutional framework.

The main point of Buchanan's public choice theory is that voluntary obedience to the "rule" of law leads to a stable social order where each individual, pursuing their own interests, leads to a distribution of wealth and income that is considered fair because citizens agreed to the creation of the constitutional rules.

The resulting emergence of a stable order occurs, after the constitution is created, when citizens engage in free market exchange to improve their own welfare.

Buchanan asserts that there is no mysterious volonté générale collective public interest or some type of macro Keynesian social welfare public purpose, independent of the interests of citizens who vote in legitimate elections.

In the third part of the book, we rely on the evolutionary economic theory of Joseph Schumpeter to describe the concept of how a free market entrepreneurial capitalist system would function, under Buchanan's constitutional rules.

The main point of Schumpeter's evolutionary economic theory is that the unfair, unequal distribution of wealth at the beginning of a constitutional period is modified, over time, to create new markets, and new distributions of wealth, that displace the initial unfair initial distribution of wealth, embedded in Madison's rules.

The new distribution of income and wealth is fair because each individual citizen has an equal opportunity, after the constitution has been created, to pursue financial prosperity, in a society where all citizens obey the rule of law.

While our book is interesting as a matter of historical interpretation of the American constitutional era, the intent of the book is not exclusively historical analysis.

We argue that Mason's concept of individual liberty would be a better pathway to form a new constitution, today, after Madison's representative republic collapsed in the corrupt election of 2020.

We begin, in Chapter 1, by explaining the historical anomaly of Mason's obscurity in scholarly documents, compared with the better known so-called "Founding Fathers."

To use a contemporary term, Mason's reputation was "cancelled" by the media of the day because he betrayed his social class allegiance to Madison's ruling class natural aristocracy.

Mason was an egalitarian who defied the peer pressure of social class consciousness of Madison's natural aristocracy, and for his opposition, he was forever cancelled by the ruling class of the day.

The fissure between Mason and the other ruling class delegates, especially with George Washington, never healed. (Henriques, Peter, An Uneven Friendship, The Virginia Magazine of History and Biography, 1989.)

The strategy for cancelling Mason, then, is the same strategy adopted today by the ruling class deep state propaganda that, "We are all in this together."

When Mason opposed Madison's document, on September 15, 1787, he demonstrated that he was not all in this together, with the other ruling class delegates.

The success of Madison's public relations strategy in implementing his constitution, was based upon the false idea that the interests of the wealthy families and corporations in America are the same as the middle and working classes.

At the very last moment of the Convention, Madison changed the wording of the Preamble from "We, the people of the assembled states," to the imaginary collective of "We, the people."

From Madison's notes: September 12.

"Committee of Style reported an amendment to Article 7, which was read by paragraph. This document (the Constitution), is preceded by a preamble, which begins, "We the People of the United States, in order to form a more perfect union…" rather than "We the people of the states of New Hampshire, etc…"

In reality, "We, the people," was only the 38 ruling class delegates who signed the document, as if those delegates virtually represented "We, the people."

Madison's strategy of using "We, the people," was successful, then, because the ruling class had a coherent social class consciousness, while the middle and working class citizens had not yet formed a social class awareness.

When the other delegates signed the document, on September 17, 1787, they had not seen, nor debated, Madison's last minute change of text in the Preamble.

After September 17, the document was transmitted in bits and pieces to the Congress of the United States, Assembled, with no instructions or procedures, from Madison, on what the Congress should do with it.

From the time the Congress obtained the draft of the document, on, or about October 15, 1787, it took about 2 more weeks for the document to be transmitted from the Congress to the 13 states for the ensuing corrupt ratification process.

Within six weeks, of November 1, 1787, five states, over half the required nine states, had ratified, not because common citizens approved of the rules, but because the ruling class aristocracy in each state was already organized in the fraudulent ratification scheme, with their coherent social class consciousness to "hurry the common citizens" into acceptance."

The constitution created by Madison was written by the members of the natural aristocracy, in a building, with doors locked and window shades pulled down.

The elites had a common social class background and a unified ideology of the aristocracy, which guided them in the creation of the constitution.

The delegates shared a common mission to overthrow the Articles of Confederation, and replace it with an unfair, and unbalanced set of rules that eliminated the threat posed to their rule by too much citizen democracy at the state government level.

The new government was not "of the people," it was government of the natural aristocracy, who obtained their very own unelected branch of government, called the Senate.

Madison knew at the time that he changed the wording in the Preamble, to "We, the people," that it was a false statement designed to deceive common citizens.

Madison had stated, early in the Convention, that his intent was to divide the society into two distinct social classes, to the benefit of the natural aristocracy.

Before he left the Convention in disgust, in June of 1787, at the plan being proposed by Madison, Robert Yates took notes on what Madison said.

From Robert Yates' notes on Madison's statement of intent,

[Quoting] Mr. Madison. We are now to determine whether the republican form shall be the basis of our government. I admit there is weight in objection of the gentleman from South Carolina [Pinckney]; but plan can steer clear of objections. That great powers [of the cental government] are to be gained, there is no doubt; and that those powers may be abused is equally true. It is also probable that members may lose their attachment the states which sent them. Yet the first branch [Senate] Will control the many [common citizens] of their abuses. But we are now forming a body on the wisdom we mean to rely, and their permanency in office secured in proper field which they may exert their firmness and knowledge. Democratic communities may be unsteady, and be led to action by impulse of the moment. Like individuals they may be sensible in their own [financial] decisions. They [common citizens] have Weakness, and may desire the counsels to guard them against the turbulency and weakness of their passions. Such are the various pursuits of this life, that in all Civil countries, the interest of a community will be divided. There will debtors and creditors, and an unequal possession of property, hence arises different views and different objects in government. indeed is the groundwork of aristocracy; and we find it blends into every government, both ancient and modem. Even where titles survived property, we discover the noble beggar haughtily assuming an equal status." (Slonim,Shlomo, Framers' Construction/Beardian Deconstruction" Essays on the Constitutional Design of 1787. Peter Lanf Pubishing, 2001.).

Madison's duplicity in using "We, the people," is belied by his stated intent to implement an aristocracy to rule over common citizens, who he refers to as, "noble beggars haughtily assuming an equal status."

The political propaganda of "We. the people,"continues to be successful, today, because the common citizens still do not have a middle class social awareness of their own economic interests, and Madison's constitution left them with no political method of removing the uni-party deep state oligarchy.

The synthesis of thought of Mason, Buchanan, and Schumpeter provides the starting point of the national debate over what form of government replaces Madison's flawed constitution.

Chapter 1. Solving the Mystery of George Mason's Obscurity in American History.

Almost every scholarly historical account of George Mason's life and accomplishments begins with a type of obligatory statement that George Mason's contribution to the creation of the nation has been overlooked and underappreciated.

One scholar, Jeff Broadwater, even titled his recent book, "George Mason: The Forgotten Founder." (UNC Press, 2006.).

After making the obligatory reference to Mason's historical obscurity, most of the historians offer explanations of why Mason has not received the recognition that he would seem to deserve.

Many of the explanations center on Mason's abrasive personality, or Mason's age, or Mason's contempt for political posturing.

The scholars who cite Mason's opposition to the document because it did not contain a Bill of Rights, generally disregard the more authentic reasons for Mason's opposition because those more authentic reasons conflict with the national narrative myth of the "founding."

We agree with the conclusion reached by John Vile, in his book, More Than A Plea For a Declaration of Rights, (Talbot Publishing, 2019.).

Vile cites Mason's draft document, of August 31, 1787, 17 days before Mason published his objections, on the last day of the Convention, related to the missing Bill of Rights.

Vile writes,

"On August 31, Mason circulated a document to some members of the Committee on Postponed Parts with a dozen proposed changes, which, if they could be obtained, would make the document "unexceptional" (this term is Madison's citd in Madison's Notes). Mason proposed the following:

- that the Council of State of from five to seven members would be appointed by two-thirds majorities in the Senate and rotate in office;
- that the "Objects of the National Government" be "*expressly* defined";
- that two-thirds, rather than three-fourths majorities of Congress should be able to override presidential vetoes;
- that navigation laws require a two-thirds vote of Congress;
- that duties on imports be uniform throughout the United States;
- that Congress should "be restrained from establishing perpetual Revenue";
- that laws for raising revenue or raising salaries [of representatives] should originate in the House of Representatives;
- that members of congress be ineligible to any offices under the national government other than military posts;
- that the president be limited to a single term;
- that treaty-making and the appointment of ambassadors require the mutual concurrence of the Senate and the Council of State;

- that the president appoint all offices created by Congress with Senate concurrence;
- that the president's power to grant pardons not extend to impeachment or treason;
- and that the Senate be prohibited from altering 'money bills

In other words, the conventional treatment of Mason's obscure reputation by the scholarly community cites the cause of his obscurity arising from either Mason's own idiosyncratic behavior, or the absence of a Bill of Rights, and not from the detailed list of objections Mason expressed during the convention, and after the convention, until he died, in 1792.

The explanation that Mason did not sign the document because it did not contain a Bill of Rights is just a politically convenient way for historians to avoid the more substantive objections Mason had with the document.

We offer an alternative explanation of Mason's historical obscurity.

We locate the cause of the obscurity in a contemporary use of political language. We argue that Mason's reputation was "cancelled," by the dominant ruling class culture of the era.

According to our explanation, the dominant social class culture of the natural aristocracy considered Mason a traitor to the social class financial and political interests of the natural aristocracy.

As Robert Rutland observed in his book, George Mason: Reluctant Statesman,

"The triumphant Federalists were not kind in their judgment of their opponents, however; even George Washington was cool toward his old friend and neighbor. Furthermore, Mason's objections to Hamiltonian consolidation gave him a black mark in the history that the partisans of the first Secretary of the Treasury did so much to write… Federalist fire was aimed mainly at Mason. Federalists would have found Patrick Henry a bigger target, but the chinks in his armor were few. Their strategy was to discredit Mason by giving prominence to every incident that might prove the master of Gunston Hall was no longer the luminary in Virginia politics he had been for so many years. In pamphlets they charged that Mason's list of objections were simply his afterthoughts." (Rutland, Robert, George Mason: Reluctant Statesman LSU Press. Kindle Edition. 1961.).

Madison called the natural aristocracy a "faction," and contrasted the natural aristocracy to the imaginary American common citizen faction.

The so-called ruling class faction had begun developing a national narrative myth about the founding of the 1787 constitution by a group of "demi-gods," who met in secret, behind closed doors, to deliver a "nearly perfect" set of constitutional rules that succeeded in overthrowing the Articles of Confederation.

Writing the true history of Mason's contributions by the scholarly community would mean going against the national narrative myth that the constitution was created by demi-gods, who were called the "founding fathers," in a single historical event called "the founding."

In contrast to the national narrative of demi-gods and a perfect constitution, Mason offered a different perspective about the men who attended the convention.

Just before the start of the Virginia ratifying convention, in June of 1788, Mason said this about his fellow delegates in Philadelphia:

"You may have been taught . . . to respect the Characters of the Members of the late Convention. You may have supposed that they were an assemblage of great men. There is nothing less true. From the Eastern States there were Knaves and Fools, from the States southward of Virginia, they were a parcel of Coxcombs and from the middle States Office Hunters not a few."

Part of the national narrative myth is that the 38 demi-gods who signed the document on September 17, 1787, were selfless, virtuous people, who put their own personal financial interests aside in order create fair rules for all citizens.

In the national narrative myth, there were not two social classes who were in conflict with each other, there was only one unified social class of, "We, the people," who all shared the same cultural values and principles of liberty.

Madison explains this part of the national narrative myth in his October 1787 letter to Jefferson, where he explains that there are not social class divisions in "We, the people."

Madison writes,

"That the people composing the society enjoy not only an equality of political rights, but that they have all precisely the same interests and the same feelings in every respect."

The success of Madison's national narrative myth was based upon the false idea in his Preamble of "We, the people," that the interests of the wealthy families and corporations in America are the same as the middle and working classes.

Madison often argued that the reason his rules insulated the agencies of government from the common citizens was because the natural aristocracy possessed personal virtue and honor.

Madison thought that common citizens could trust the fairness of the rules because the natural aristocracy would base their decisions on what was best for the common citizens.

In other words, because the natural aristocracy possessed the moral value of virtue, they knew better what was good for the common citizens than the common citizens themselves, and further, that the common citizens could trust the elites to make the best decisions.

Hamilton's descriptive term for the common citizens was "howling masses," which highlights the fact that the natural aristocracy had both a coherent class awareness of their own financial interests, as well as a unified class awareness of the social class characteristics of common citizens.

Edward Rutledge, a delegate from South Carolina, expressed his disgust of common citizens from the North.

During the Convention, speaking about common citizens, Rutledge said,

"their low cunning and those leveling principles, which men without character and without fortunes, in general which are so captivating to the lower class of mankind." (Pacheco, Josephine, Ed., Antifederalism: The Legacy of George Mason, , George Mason University Press, 1992.).

The authentic perspective of the natural aristocracy about elite rule was provided, in 1788, by Jonathan Jackson, in his book, Thoughts Upon The Political Situation in the United States.

Jackson wrote,

"A natural aristocracy that had to dominate public authority in order to prevent America from degenerating into a democratic licentiousness, into a government where the people would be directed by no rule but their own will and caprice...Tyranny by the people was the worst kind because it left few resources to the oppressed [the oppressed are the natural aristocracy.]" (Jackson, Jonathan. Thoughts Upon the Political Situation of the United States of America: In which that of Massachusetts is More Particularly Considered. With Some Observations on the Constitution for a Federal Government. Addressed to the People of the Union, 1788.).

John Dickinson a delegate at the convention from Delaware stated,

"The US Senate would combine the families and wealth of aristocracy in order to establish a check on Democracy...the new constitution must protect "the worthy against the licentious...the Federal constitution placed the remedy in the hands of the well born, which feel the disorder of democracy, whereas the antifederalists placed the remedy in the hands of citizens (the common people), who cause the disorder."

James Wilson, a delegate to the convention from Pennsylvania, stated,

"The inferior order of the people [are different]...the elites were born a different race from them...the rest of mankind were born to serve to administer food to the ambition of their superiors and become the footstool of their power." (Klarman,Michael, The Framers Coup, Oxford University Press, 2016.).

For the community of scholars, since that time, in order to elevate Mason to his rightful historical significance would mean that historians were transgressing the national narrative myth about the founding of the nation by selfless, virtuous men.

As a way around questioning the national narrative myth, the community of historians have located part of the cause of Mason's obscurity in his own behavior.

Their treatment of Mason continues the politically correct history of canceling Mason, rather than questioning the historical accuracy of the national narrative myth.

With some exceptions, historians today continue to use the accepted ruling class terminology that Mason was an "anti-federalist," rather than the more accurate description that Mason was a state sovereignty egalitarian.

In the conventional historical usage of the myth, the term "anti-federalist" meant that Mason was against the progress of the improvements that the ruling class aristocracy wanted to obtain in overthrowing the state sovereignty framework of the Articles of Confederation with a consolidated powerful central government.

The historically misnamed "Federalists" cast themselves as the progressive forces that were trying to overcome the defects of the Articles of Confederation.

The accurate definition of "federalist," would be a person in favor of decentralized state sovereignty.

Historians today continue to deploy this false terminology as a part of continuing the national narrative myth.

From their unified social class awareness, the ruling class promoted the public relations propaganda that the Articles were defective, and the Federalists were trying to fix the defects with a new powerful central government.

There are two interpretations of the question whether the Articles of Confederation were defective, beyond repair.

From the perspective of the common citizens, the Articles, and the framework of state sovereignty were not defective.

As Philanthropos, a state sovereignty patriot, wrote in 1788,

"Our present constitution, (the Articles), with a few additional powers to Congress, seems better calculated to preserve the rights and defend the liberties of our citizens, than the one proposed, (by Madison), without proper amendments. Let us therefore, for once, show our judgment and solidity by continuing it, (the Articles), and prove the opinion to be erroneous, that levity and fickleness are not only the foibles of our society."

In Federalists and Antifederalists: The Debate Over the Ratification of the Constitution, John Kaminsky and Richard Leffler, cite the article " What is your condition," [under the articles?]from A Plebian, who states that the lives of common citizens under the Articles of Confederation were good.

"What is your condition? Does not every man sit under his own vine and under his own fig-tree, having none to make him afraid? Does not every one follow his calling without impediments and receive the reward of his well-earned industry? The farmer cultivates his land, and reaps the fruit which the bounty of heaven bestows on his honest toil. The mechanic is exercised in his art, and receives the reward of his labour. The merchant drives his commerce, and none can deprive him of the gain he honestly acquires; all classes and callings of men amongst us are protected in their various pursuits, and secured by the laws in the possession and enjoyment of the property-obtained in those pursuits: The laws are as well executed as they ever were, in this or any other country. Neither the hand of private violence, nor the more to be dreaded hand of legal oppression, are reached out to distress us." (Madison House, 1998.).

From the perspective of the ruling class, the Articles were defective, beyond repair.

For historians, it is intellectually easier and politically correct to write American history from the perspective of the national narrative of the natural aristocracy that the Articles were defective.

Angelo Codevilla correctly applied the historical national narrative myth to contemporary times.

Codevilla wrote,

"The elite's attitude (of moral superiority) is key to understanding our bipartisan ruling class. Its first tenet is that "we" (the elites) are the best and brightest while the rest of Americans are retrograde, racist, and dysfunctional, unless properly constrained…Our ruling class's agenda is power for itself." (Codevilla, Angelo The Ruling Class: How They Corrupted America and What We Can Do About It, Beaufort Books, 2010.).

The perspective of the ruling class was dominant, then, as it is today, and it explains why the historical community continues to cancel the reputation of George Mason.

In their book, "The Five George Masons: Patriots and Planters of Virginia and Maryland," Pamela Copeland and Richard MacMaster, cite the obscurity of his death, in 1792. (University of Virginia Press, 1975.).

They write,

"His [Mason's] death went virtually unnoticed perhaps because his national politics had been so strongly anti-federalist."

Josephine Pacheco, writing in The Legacy of George Mason, states,

"In the history of the Revolution, however, Mason never received his deserved recognition, and consequently he has become an almost forgotten man in the pantheon of revolutionary heroes." (George Mason University Press, 1983.).

In her book, "George Mason: Gentleman Revolutionary," Helen Hill Miller, writes,

"Down through the years, George Mason's contribution to the constitution-making period, state and national has been relatively little recognized…his name tended to be lost to sight." (UNC Press, 1975.).

William G. Hyland, Jr., writing in "George Mason: The Founding Father Who Gave Us The Bill of Rights," states,

"Mason lost the friendship of Washington and others [natural aristocracy] over his refusal to endorse the document [constitution] in its final form. His refusal cost him his rightful place in the annals of history to some extent, as well. Mason is sometimes referred to as the "Forgotten Founder," largely ignored by history books and often uncredited for originating many of the core concepts and much of the language later incorporated in both the Declaration of Independence and the Bill of Rights…Mason demanded that the delegates [at the convention] attend to the rights of every class of people." (Regnery History, 2019.).

In "George Mason and the Legacy of Constitutional Liberty: An Examination of the Influence of George Mason on the American Bill of Rights," Donald Senese, asks,

"Why isn't George Mason better known?...Why can you watch an informative film at the Visitor's Center in Philadelphia and hear not a mention of George Mason's name?" (Fairfax County History Commission, 1989.).

Margaret Stimmann Bransom speculates that Mason's obscurity is related to three factors. She writes,

It is hard to explain why George Mason has not attained the status of a cultural icon that Americans have bestowed on his Virginia colleagues such as George Washington, Thomas Jefferson, and James Madison… Why, then, is Mason less celebrated as a "Founding Father" and as a "Framer of the Constitution"?... First, most Americans know little about him, except that he refused to sign the Constitution when it was completed at the Philadelphia Convention in 1787. They are unaware of his reasons for refusing to sign. They do not know the important role he played in seeing that the Bill of Rights were added to the Constitution by the First Congress in 1791…A second reason is that all but a very modest number of his papers have disappeared, hindering the work of would-be biographers and interested citizens…A third reason may stem from Mason's personal characteristics. Mason did not suffer fools gladly. Patience was not one of his hallmarks. He has been described as "the sharp-spoken planter."

(Branson, Margaret Stimmann, George Mason: The Reluctant Founder, Center for Civic Education. ND.).

Dumas Malone, writing in the Foreword of Robert Rutland's book, "George Mason: Reluctant Statesman," states,

"The fact that Jefferson rather than Mason became the major American symbol of individual freedom and personal rights is attributable to no difference between the two men in basic philosophy, but was owing rather to the subsequent course of events and the accidents of history…The triumphant Federalists were not kind in their judgment of their opponents, however; even George Washington was cool toward his old friend and neighbor. Furthermore, Mason's objections to Hamiltonian consolidation gave him a black mark in the history the partisans of the first Secretary of the Treasury did so much to write. (Rutland, Robert A., George Mason: Reluctant Statesman, 1961.).

The internet website, History on the Net, writes, in "George Mason: The Most Important Founding Father Nobody Remembers,"

"But his contribution has been obscured by accidents of history and his self effacing character… his name lost to public fame…buried in almost two and a half centuries of public oblivion...History has consigned Mason to the second tier of Founders." (Salem Media. September, 2022.).

Broadwater begins his work trying to explain why Mason has been overlooked by the academic community of scholars.

He writes,

"The small community of Mason scholars has occasionally attempted to explain its subject's relative obscurity …it is explained by his own reluctance to seek the historical spotlight." ("George Mason: The Forgotten Founder," (UNC Press, 2006.).

On its website, the Scalia Law School, at George Mason University, in their introductory text on Mason, titled, "George Mason, the Man," notes,

"The fact is unquestionable, that the Virginia Bill of Rights, and the Constitution of Virginia, were drawn originally by George Mason, one of our greatest men, and of the first order of greatness. His refusal to sign the document [on September 17, 1787], cost him his rightful place in the annals of history to some extent, as well. Mason is sometimes referred to as the "Forgotten Founder," and is largely ignored by history books and often uncredited for originating many of the core concepts and much of the language later incorporated in both the [Jefferson's] Declaration of Independence and the [1791], Bill of Rights."

We offer a different explanation of Mason's historical obscurity.

Mason was a radical egalitarian, who defied the social class allegiance of the natural aristocracy to oppose Madison's implementation of the British social class structure in America.

Mason's son described his father's egalitarianism, by writing,

"George Mason set the highest example of a free-born and liberty loving American citizen by meeting all men on the level of their intrinsic mental and moral worth without regard to their wealth, social standing or political station." (Mason, Robert C., George Mason of Virginia, Oscar Aurlius Morgner, 1919.).

It was Mason's egalitarian, individualistic ideology that caused Mason to be cancelled by the Ruling Class elite.

In his article, "Yes! No! and If!" Jon Kukla writes that the natural aristocracy was shocked by Mason's democratic anti- ruling class ideology.

Kukla writes,

"Mason's formidable task was made more difficult by the many people who were "schock'd at the monstrous absurdity of supposing that such characters as Washington and Franklin, who, by a long life of virtue and patriotism, have acquired reputations not to be extinguished but with the world, should not, in their old age, with their mental faculties unimpaired, lend the sanction of their names to establish a system of [aristocratic] tyranny!" (Kukla, Jon, Yes! No! and If!, internet blog article, ND.).

We agree with the analysis of Helen Hill, in her 1966 book, "George Mason: Constitutionalist," that Mason was a social aristocrat, but extend her analysis to add that it was the unified and coherent social class ideology of the ruling class as the explanation for why the natural aristocracy cancelled Mason.

Mason was a Virginia aristocrat who betrayed his social class membership in the natural aristocracy.

In the Forgotten Founder, Broadwater writes,

"Forty or so wealthy families dominated Virginia politics…[appointed] political positions such as justice of the peace were passed down from father to son, from uncle to nephew.

In George Mason: Gentleman Revolutionary, Helen Hill Miller, cites the sociological work of JFD Smyth, who wrote,

"Virginia social structure [has] three degrees of rank…exclusive of the negroes. the first are gentlemen of the best families…These in general have had a liberal education, possess enlightened understandings, and a thorough knowledge of the world, that furnishes them with an ease and freedom of manners and conversation, highly to their advantage in exterior, which no vicissitude of fortune or place can divest them of; they being actually, according to my ideas, the most agreeable and best companions, friends, and neighbours, that need be desired..
…Those of the second degree in rank are very numerous, being perhaps half the inhabitants ... they are generous, friendly, and hospitable in the extreme; but mixed with

Such an appearance of rudeness, ferocity, and haughtiness, which is in tad only a want, of polish…Many of them possess fortunes superior to some of the first rank, but their families are not so ancient, nor respectable; a circumstance here held in some estimiation…The third, or lower class of the people (who, ever compose the bulk of mankind), are in Virginia more few in number, in proportion to the rest of the inhabitants than perhaps in any other Country in the universe. Even these are kind, hospitable, and generous; yet illiberal, noisy, and rude... " (UNC Press, 1975.).

In Wirt's "Sketches of the Life and Character of Patrick Henry", about Virginia's social class structure, Wirt wrote,

"There were, then, first, aristocrats, composed of the great land holders who had seated themselves below tide water on the main rivers, and lived in a style of luxury and extravagance, insupportable by the other inhabitants, and which, indeed, ended, in several instances, in the ruin of their own fortunes. Next to these were what might be called half breeds; the descendants of the younger sons and daughters of the aristocrats, who inherited the pride of their ancestors without their wealth. Then came the pretenders, men who from vanity or the impulse of growing wealth or from that enterprize which is natural to talents, sought to detach themselves from the plebeian ranks, to which they properly belonged, and imitated, at some distance, the manners and habits of the great. Next to these, were a solid and independent yeomanry, looking askance at those above, yet not venturing to jostle them. And last and lowest, a fecuium of beings called overseers, the most abject, degraded, unprincipled race, always cap in hand to the dons who employed them, and furnishing materials for the exercise of their pride, insolence, and spirit of domination." (Wirt, William Sketches of the Life and Character of Patrick Henry, Andrus Hartford, & Son, 1852.).

In "The Constitutional Convention of 1787: A Biographical Dictionary," Joseph C. Morton, writes about the social class unity of the natural aristocracy. He writes,

"[The aristocracy was] from the uppermost economic, political, and social strata of American society…they were an exceedingly homogeneous group regarding most economic, social and political matters." (Greenwood Press, 2006.).

Helen Hill writes that Mason was a member of this Virginia aristocracy,

"His personal life as a private gentleman followed the aristocratic agricultural pattern of the past, his public life as a constitutionalist and practical legislator gave form to the democratic values of the future….The extent to which the democratic revolution in Virginia was the work of aristocrats…in relation to democracy, it was an innovation from which the chief innovators had nothing material to gain…(selfless) The tidewater sheltered an established system of production an aristocratic social order, an accumulated capital, and a creditor position…the family, property, the county, and the church all contributed to a corporate sense of society…[with] a high value on [social] order." (George Mason: Constitutionalist, 1966.).

If Mason had simply offended other individual aristocrats with his egalitarian philosophy, his contribution to history would not have been cancelled.

But, he did not confront and offend individual aristocrats with his egalitarian ideas, he offended a unified, coherent social order of the elites, and it was opposing the peer pressure of this consolidated power of the elites that cancelled Mason for his betrayal of their social class interests.

The members of the American aristocracy knew each other, and had worked together, as a group, from 1774 to 1787.

In The Other Founders, Saul Cornell, explains that 34 of the 38 signers of the constitution had also worked together during the Continental and Confederation Congresses. (UNC Press, 1999.).

They were: Johnson, Sherman, Bedford, Dickinson, Read, Few, Baldwin, Carroll, Jennifer, McHenry, Gorham, King, Gilman, Langdon, Hamilton, Dayton, Livingston, Paterson, Blount, Williamson, Spaight, Clymer, Fitssimons, Franklin, Ingersoll, Mifflin, Morris, Morris, Wilson, Butler, Pinckney, Rutledge, Madison, Washington.

The 34 delegates were self-selected, or appointed by other elites, to attend the convention. Not one of the delegates at the Convention could be considered a common citizen.

The only delegate who represented the financial and political interests of common citizens at the convention was George Mason, himself a member of the natural aristocracy.

Mason's historical obscurity is not simply and solely his refusal to sign Madison's document.

His opposition was based upon his view that Madison's attempt to replicate the social class political conflict model in England would result in a corrupt and venal social system in America.

The unified and coherent social class awareness of the aristocracy in America was based upon the shared understanding that it was their social class financial connections to the British aristocracy that had rewarded their financial interests.

In order to preserve their social class privileges, Madison intended to replicate the British social class conflict model in America.

Merrill Jensen quotes Gouverneur Morris, a delegate from New York, who wrote, in 1774,

"That the British connection was the guarantee of the existing aristocratic order"

In Jensen's book, he writes that after the revolution, they [the aristocrats] engaged with conservatives [elites] in other states in undoing the Articles of Confederation." (Jensen, Merrill, The Articles of Confederation, University of Wisconsin Press, 1970.).

Madison's "more perfect union," was a replication of the British social class conflict model, where America's natural aristocracy would obtain the same kind of benefits and privileges as the British ruling classes.

Writing about Madison's constitution, in 1890, Christopher Tiedman describes the similarity of Madison's rules to the British social class conflict model of government.

Tiedman writes,

"Where ever there was no contest [between the delegates], the English precedents were followed…the President was an imitation of King George…the Senate corresponded to the House of Lords, and the House [of Representatives] to the House of Commons…the American constitution was an evolutionary growth out of the British constitution." (The Unwritten Constitution of the United States: A Philosophical Inquiry Into the Fundamentals of American Constitutional Law, G. P. Putnam, 1890.).

Brent Tarter, writing in The Virginia Magazine of History and Biography, states,

"In the opinion of Mason…imperfections in the structure of the British government had undermined the once sound principles of the British constitution and allowed corruption to disrupt or destroy the well-balanced system that mixed the three estates of society [royalty, nobility and commons] in a government of interlocking executive, legislative and judicial institutions. (George Mason and the Conservation of Liberty, July, 1991.).

Mason spoke during the Virginia ratification convention, of 1788, and stated,

"We are not indeed constituting a British Government, but a more dangerous monarchy, an elective one."

In A Politics of Tensions: The Articles of Confederation and American Political Ideas, Robert Hoffert, quotes Thomas Paine, who stated,

"The US Constitution of 1787 is an ill-advised attempt to replicate the British form of mixed constitution...Their basis for justice becomes the balancing of particular class interests [factions]....they make it difficult for citizens to participate." (University Press of Colorado, 1992.).

During the Virginia ratifying convention, of 1788, speaking in opposition to ratification, James Monroe cited the differences between the authentic British social class political system and the truncated version that Madison created in his constitution.

Monroe said:

"The English constitution is based upon social orders which have a repellent quality which enabled it to preserve itself from being destroyed by the other [social classes]. The American division of power [in Madison] has no such basis and, indeed, no such intention. There are no real checks in the Constitution that would prevent a coalition of the branches of government and encroachments on the rights of the people." (Vass, Laurie Thomas, After the Collapse of America: The Democratic Republic of America, Gabby Press, 2019.).

In The Articles of Confederation, Merrill Jensen, describes the rampant corruption of the natural aristocracy in colonial Virginia and North Carolina, which was clearly evident to Mason, and served as the basis of his opposition to Madison's British social class rules.

Jensen writes,

"Virginia's aristocracy ran the colony for their own particular benefit, they embezzled public funds, and they used their control of the legislature to further their speculative schemes in Virginia's vast western territory…In North Carolina, the royal governor appointed sheriffs and court officials. This made it possible for a system of corruption and extortion unequaled in the other 12 colonies….if the farmers had no ready money to pay their taxes, their property was sold…[After 1787]. When the aristocracy gained control of the state, after 10 years of radical rule, they united with aristocrats in other states in overturning the Articles of Confederation. (University of Wisconsin Press, 1970.).

Jensen quotes Richard Henry Lee, in 1788, about Madison's implementation of the British social class conflict model in America.

Lee states,

"It will be considered, I believe, as a most extraordinary epoch in the history of mankind, that in a few years there should be so essential a change in the minds of men. Tis really astonishing that the same people who have just emerged from a long and cruel war in defence of liberty, should now agree to fix an elective despotism upon themselves and their posterity."

In the corrupt system in Great Britain, ordinary common citizens did not have a fair chance for financial success, and this absence of equal opportunity galled Mason.

Joseph Schumpeter, in Capitalism, Socialism, and Democracy, accurately described the American ruling class as an "oligarchy." The class consciousness that Schumpeter described was based upon a shared set of cultural and social values, or as Schumpeter stated, "sharing the right socio-political opinions." (Harper Perennial, 1962.).

Schumpeter explains that membership in the American ruling class is tightly controlled by self-enforced social rules.

Citizens from the middle class and underclass are rarely, if ever, admitted into the ruling oligarchy.

In his book, Who rules America? Power and Politics in the Year 2006, William Domhoff describes his research in documenting the elements of the American ruling class.

Domhoff states that his research shows,

"First, it shows there is a nationwide social upper class in the United States that has its own exclusive social institutions and is based in the ownership of great wealth. Second, it demonstrates that this upper class is closely intertwined with the corporate community. Third, it argues that the social cohesion that develops among members' of the upper class is another basis for the creation of policy agreements within the policy-formation network. The demonstration of an upper class that is tightly interconnected with the corporate community is relevant because it contradicts the idea that there has been a separation between corporate ownership and control in the United States." (Routledge, 8th edition, 2021.).

Domhoff cites the importance of social class awareness among members of the ruling class in maintaining social and political control.

His term for their power is "class dominance."

He writes,

"Involvement in these institutions usually instills a class consciousness that includes feelings of superiority, pride, and justified privilege. Deep down, most members of the upper class think they are better than other people and therefore fully deserving of their station in life—an attitude that is very useful in managing employees, even though it is sometimes psychologically debilitating. This class consciousness is ultimately based in the society-wide categories of owners and nonowners, but it is reinforced by the shared social identities and interpersonal ties created by participation in social institutions of the upper class." (2021.).

Max Weber's social class conflict theory posits that there are three main sources of conflict: economic, social, and political. This theory focuses on the competition between social groups, [factions] rather than individuals, and attempts to explain social change and stability as a result of group conflict.

In this view, social order is maintained by domination and power rather than by consensus and voluntary citizen obedience to the rule of law.

Rhonda Levine, in Social Class and Stratification: Classic Statements and Theoretical Debates, defines social class as a number of people who share similar experiences, social networks, and status in the social structure. She states that class refers to a status group and a basis of social action. (Rowman & Littlefield, 2006.).

To cite Angelo Codevilla (2010) again, the American ruling class shares common beliefs and attitudes, education, family, money, character and morals. The ruling class has a shared consciousness of the world, and the type of political economic system that will benefit their social class.

We argue that Madison's ruling class, in 1787, had a social class awareness of their own interests as well as a commonly held view about common citizens.

The natural aristocracy was well-organized and well-funded, and they had a coherent social class consciousness, derived from working with each other from 1774 to 1787.

The sociological factor of social class awareness of Madison's natural aristocracy explains how and why the American constitution was created and evolved.

The tiny financial faction of the American natural aristocracy, in 1787, had an ideological framework, and the financial resources to implement their cultural values in Madison's convention.

The natural aristocracy had the social and political power to cancel Mason's reputation. The natural aristocracy considered Mason to be a traitor to their cause and they had the collective power to cancel him.

In contrast to the ruling class consciousness, the financial interests and political cultural values of the common citizens were not organized politically, and those social interests were not rich enough to fund their own social class awareness political agenda, even if they had actually created a social class consciousness.

Consequently, Madison's ruling class did not have ideological competition at the Convention, and the elites wrote the rules to benefit their own social and financial interests.

And, following Buchanan, the common citizens were never granted the opportunity to provide consent, or to withdraw original consent, as if that consent had actually been obtained in the corrupt ratification process.

It took Madison 4 weeks to transmit the text to the Congress, and several weeks for the Congress to transmit the document, with no further instructions on what the states should do.

Within 3 months of October 17, 1787, 5 states had already ratified the Constitution in the corrupt ratification process, without further public debate or discussion.

- Delaware: December 7, 1787.
- Pennsylvania: December 12, 1787.
- New Jersey: December 18, 1787.
- Georgia: January 2, 1788.
- Connecticut: January 9, 1788.

Common citizens in those states never had a chance to defeat the constitution, primarily because common citizens were disorganized politically, and did not have a coherent class awareness of their own financial interests.

Those citizens were never given a choice between Madison's document, or some other document, like the Articles of Confederation.

The public relations campaign of the Federalists, before the Convention was that its purpose was to revise the Articles, not to stage a coup.

As Mason said during the last days of the convention, the choice given to common citizens was "take this or nothing."

In the one state that allowed citizens to vote on ratification, the citizens voted 98% against ratification, an accurate reflection of how common citizens in all 13 states viewed Madison's document.

The only element of on-going consent in Madison's constitution was the citizen's ability to vote every four years on the uni-party elites who will rule them.

And, that last shred of legitimate citizen consent was eradicated in the Democrat Marxist coup, of 2020, in a sham election process called ballot harvesting.

And, without legitimate citizen consent, there is no longer Madison's representative republic.

On the last day of the Convention, on September 17, 1787, Mason predicted that Madison's rules would end either in an aristocracy, or a monarchy, but he could not predict which outcome was most likely.

Mason wrote,

"This government will set out a moderate aristocracy: it is at present impossible to foresee whether it will, in its operation, produce a monarchy, or a corrupt, tyrannical aristocracy; it will most probably vibrate some years between the two, and then terminate in the one or the other."

With the benefit of hindsight of the 2020 presidential election, we can now answer definitively that Madison's government ended in a corrupt tyrannical aristocracy, which is entirely disconnected from the consent of the governed.

The modern political term for the current American centralized ruling class aristocracy is deep state oligarchy.

The pathway out of the oligarchy is to rehabilitate Mason's historical reputation, as the most important founding father, and to revive Mason's vision of state sovereignty egalitarianism, in a new constitution, that replaces

Madison's flawed British social class competition model of government.

Chapter 2. Mason's Egalitarian Principles of Individual Rights and His Concept of the State Sovereignty Constitutional Framework of Liberty.

Mason had an individualist perspective on natural rights, derived from his understanding of John Locke's philosophy that rights inured to individual citizens, not to group collectives of different social classes.

According to Helen Hill, in George Mason: Constitutionalist,

"Mason follows Locke's idea that man in subscribing to the social compact, gives up only a part of this rights...that the individual reserved to himself certain powers." (Hill, Helen, George Mason: Constitutionalist, Peter Smith Edition,1966.).

In his book about Mason, Robert Rutland cites John Locke as the source of Mason's individualist philosophy.

Rutland writes,

[Mason believed] "that men are entitled to the means of acquiring and possessing property marked an historic advance from John Locke's trilogy of rights—life, liberty, and property—that simply endorsed ownership of property...Contained within it was an unlimited faith in free men to make the proper decision under any circumstances. A government is the creation of the people, who can maintain or abolish it—whichever they choose. This was not philosophical speculation, an hypothesis for quiet, fireside analysis. It was a course of action." (Rutland, Robert A., George Mason: Reluctant Statesman, LSU Press. Kindle Edition. 1961).

Rutland makes the important point that Mason extended Locke's proviso on unlimited property in the state of nature, to the additional principle, in Mason, that citizens have a right to both acquire, and a right to use property, to advance their own prosperity.

Josephine Pacheco, in Antifederalism: The Legacy of George Mason, (George Mason University Press, 1992.) writes,

"Drawing on principles expressed in John Locke's Letter Concerning Toleration, Mason included an article on religion in the "first draught" of the Virginia Declaration. His original proposal declared: That as Religion, or the Duty which we owe to our divine and omnipotent Creator, and the Manner of discharging it, can be governed only by Reason and Conviction, not by Force or Violence; and therefore that all Men shou'd enjoy the fullest Toleration in the Exercise of Religion, according to the Dictates of Conscience, unpunished and unrestrained by the Magistrate, unless, under Colour of Religion, any Man disturb the Peace, the Happiness, or Safety of Society, or of Individuals. And that it is the mutual Duty of all, to practice Christian forbearance, Love and Charity towards Each other."

Pacheco makes the important distinction in Mason's philosophy, between mere "religious toleration," which allows a state established church to collect taxes on behalf of the church, and religious liberty, which both Madison and Mason embraced in their creation of the Virginia state Constitution..

Pacheco writes,

"Historically speaking, religious *toleration* is to be contrasted with religious liberty. The former often assumes an established church and is always a revocable grant of the civil state rather than a natural, unalienable right. In Madison's mind, the right of religious exercise was too important to be cast in the form of a mere privilege allowed by the ruling civil polity and enjoyed as a grant of governmental benevolence. Rather, he viewed religious liberty as a natural and unalienable right, possessed equally by all citizens, which must be beyond the reach of civil magistrates."

In his 1775 address to the assembled militia in Fairfax County, Virginia, Mason said,

"We came equals into this world, and equals shall we go out of it. All men are by nature born equally free and independent. To protect the weaker from the injuries and insults of the stronger were societies first formed; when men entered into compacts to give up some of their natural rights, that by union and mutual assistance they might secure the rest; but they gave up no more than the nature of the thing required. Every society, all government, and every kind of civil impact therefore, is or ought to be, calculated for the general good and safety of the community. Every power, every authority vested in particular men is, or ought to be, ultimately directed to this sole end; and whenever any power or authority whatever extends further, or is of longer duration than is in its nature necessary for these purposes, it may be called government, but it is in fact oppression."

Much of the historical commentary about Mason's views on individual natural rights are combined and conjoined to his principles of a constitutional framework of liberty, in a democratic, decentralized government.

This treatment of the topic of the primacy of Mason's methodological individualism by academic historians shifts the historical focus to the less important topic of Mason's refusal to sign Madison's document.

The two topics, individualism and the constitutional framework of liberty, are distinct and separate, but the academic community combines both topics into their explanation of Mason's obscurity in history in order to make their point that the most important explanation for Mason's obscurity is tied to his refusal to sign Madison's document because it did not have a Bill of Rights.

This combination of the three topics into one argument about Mason's opposition during the Convention is a politically correct way for historians to obscure the intellectual merit of Mason's natural rights philosophy of individualism, in favor of the more academically fashionable group identity collectivism.

Mason was both the author of the Virginia Declaration of Rights on the principles of individual rights, and the first constitution of Virginia, on the liberty framework of government, both written in 1776.

Those two events in history, the Declaration of Rights and the Virginia Constitution, occurred 11 years before Mason refused to sign the document, and 12 years before Mason appeared in the Virginia ratification convention to oppose Madison's rules.

Long before Mason wrote those two documents, he had authored other documents, like the 1775 address to the Fairfax Militia, where he explained his philosophy of natural rights and the framework of a decentralized, democratic citizen participatory government.

In Mason's Fairfax Resolves, written by both George Washington and George Mason on July 17, 1774, they write,

"The Claim lately assumed and exercised by the British Parliament, of making such Laws as they think fit, to govern the People of these Colonies, [virtual representation] and to extort from us our Money without our Consent, is not only diametrically contrary to the first Principles of the [unwritten British] Constitution, and the original Compacts [Magna Carta, 1215] by which we are dependant upon the British Crown and Government; but is totally incompatible with the Privileges of a free People, and the natural Rights of Mankind. . . .Taxation and Representation are in their Nature inseperable; . . . the Right of withholding, or of giving and granting their own Money is the only effectual Security to a free People, against the Encroachments of Despotism and Tyranny; and that whenever they yield the One, they must quickly fall a Prey to the other…but tho' we are it's Subjects, [of the King] we will use every Means which Heaven bath given us to prevent our becoming it's Slaves." (Miller, Helen Hill George Mason : Gentleman Revolutionary, UNC Press, 1975.).

William G. Hyland, Jr., in George Mason: The Founding Father Who Gave Us The Bill of Rights, (Regnery History, 2019), cites the main principles of individual liberty in the Fairfax Resolves.

Hyland writes,

- "That the colonists were entitled to all of the "rights, immunities and privileges which are enjoyed by those who live within the realm of England." The colonists are not a conquered people.
- That people cannot be governed by laws for which they have not given their consent.
- That Americans are not represented in the British Parliament; [virtual representation] therefore they can be subject only to those laws enacted by their own provincial assemblies or Parliaments.
- That taxation and representation go hand-in-hand; therefore, without representation the colonists cannot be taxed by the British Parliament…Mason concluded the Fairfax Resolves with an especially hard-hitting paragraph:
- Resolved that the powers over the people of America now claimed by the British House of Commons, in whose election we have no share, on whose determinations we can have no influence, whose

information must be always defective and often false...and who are removed from those impressions of tenderness and compassion arising from personal intercourse and connections, which soften the rigours of the most despotic governments, must—if continued, establish the most grievous and intolerable species of tyranny and oppression that ever was inflicted upon mankind."

The common theme to all Mason's early documents was Mason's life-long opposition to the corruption inherent in the British social class competition model of government, that elevated the interests of the nobility over the interests of common citizens.

The singular most important explanation for Mason's refusal to sign Madison's document is that Madison's rules replicated the corrupt British form of government in America, which violated the reasons why American citizens had fought against the British king in the Revolution.

Copeland and MacMaster write,

"Mason was an advocate of democracy, not because he held some romantic notion of the inherent goodness of man, but because he feared the inherent tendency to evil in every man, a tendency most dangerous in those who held power by reason of their public office." (Copeland, Pamela and MacMaster, Richard, The Five George Masons: Patriots and Planters of Virginia and Maryland. University of Virginia Press, 1975.).

Mason understood that the underlying logic of Madison's rules in replicating the British mixed government form of power was based upon the American ruling class's financial benefits, gained from their economic banking and trading relationships with the British nobility.

In More Than A Plea For a Declaration of Rights, John Vile explains that Mason was acutely aware that the British mixed social class competition form of government would lead to a corrupt American version in Madison's replication of British political rules. (Talbot Publishing, 2019.).

Vile writes,

"One reason that Mason was so concerned about both aristocracy and tyranny was that he had a clear sense that families, including his own, who were privileged in one generation could easily lose their class status. During the opening days of the Convention (May 31), in lauding the House of Representatives and his hope that it would be "the grand depository of the democratic principle of the Govt" (Farrand, 48), Mason had thus observed that "We ought to attend to the rights of every class of the people." He further noted during the Convention, that: He had often wondered at the indifference of the superior classes of society to this dictate of humanity & policy, considering that however affluent their circumstances, or elevated their situations, might be, the course of a few years, not only might but certainly would, distribute their posterity throughout the lowest classes of Society. Every selfish motive therefore, every family attachment, ought to recommend such a system of policy as would provide no less carefully for the rights and happiness of the lowest than of the highest orders of citizens. (notes from Farrand, 1: 49). Farrand, Max, ed.. The Records of the Federal Convention of 1787. 4 vols. Yale University Press, 1966.).

On the last day of the Convention, Mason correctly predicted, that once that corrupt British social class model of power was embedded into the Constitution, it would become a permanent feature of American society, leading to a corrupt centralized American ruling class, culminating in the corrupt election of 2020, when Madison's rules finally succeeded in achieving his vision of "totally excluding citizens from participating in government."

In his philosophy of equal natural rights, Mason was an egalitarian. He saw each individual citizen equally endowed with God-given rights. In social matters, Mason envisioned a certain type of mutuality in respect among citizens, not encumbered by a person's wealth or income.

During the Convention of 1787, when the foes of the common citizens were attempting to establish income and property criteria for voting or holding elected office, Mason stated,

"Does nothing besides property mark a permanent attachment [to the government]? … They [the natural aristocracy] view non-property citizens as suspicious characters and unworthy to be trusted with the common rights of their fellow citizens."

Pecheco quotes Mason's statement, made two years before Jefferson wrote the Declaration of Independence,

"By God and Nature, vested in, and consequently derived from the People, magistrates [agents of the government] were their Trustees and Servants. Government existed for the common Benefit and Security of the People, Nation, or Community, and when it no longer served that purpose a Majority of the Community had an indubitable, inalienable and indefeasible Right to reform,, alter or abolish it"

(Pacheco, Josephine ed., The Legacy of George Mason, George Mason University Press, 1983.).

The mutuality of respect among citizens influenced Mason's principles of reciprocity in the defense of liberty, once citizens had agreed to leave the state of nature in order to better secure their liberties.

In other words, the two parts of Mason's philosophy of individual natural rights were mutuality and reciprocity among citizens.

When they left the state of nature, citizens absorbed a civil obligation to other citizens to defend encroachments on liberty, either by agents of the state, or, more importantly, from social class political privileges of the natural aristocracy that were not derived from the consent of the governed.

As Michael Zuckert noted in his writings about Jefferson,

"We come to respect those rights in others which we value in ourselves. Rights in the proper sense arise when human beings come to recognize a need for reciprocity in rights…that to claim a right for oneself requires accepting the same right in others…claims of rights become rights with duties reciprocal to them." (Zuckert, Michael, The Natural Rights Republic: Studies In The Foundation of The American Political Tradition, University of Notre Dame Press, 1996..

Daniel Driesbach writes that The Virginia Declaration opened with these words:

"That all men are by nature equally free and independent, and have certain inherent rights, of which, when they enter into a state of society, they cannot, by any compact, deprive or divest their posterity; namely, the enjoyment of life and liberty, with the means of acquiring and possessing property, and pursuing and obtaining happiness and safety." (Driesbach, Daniel, George Mason's Pursuit of Religious Liberty in Revolutionary Virginia. Gunston Gazette, Vol. 2, No. 2, 1997.).

Driesbeck continues,

"Among the important principles set forth in the Declaration are these:
- That all power is derived from the people and that government officials are their trustees and servants.
- That no government official is entitled to a hereditary office.
- That the legislative, executive and judicial branches of government should be separate from one another.

- That freedom of the press is a "bulwark of liberty."
- That free exercise of religion is a right to which all are entitled.
- That standing armies in time of peace should be avoided as dangerous to liberty. At all times the military should be under civilian control.

There is a great historical continuity between the principles that Hyland cites in the Fairfax Resolves, and the principles that Driesbeck cites in the Virginia Declaration of Rights.

We argue that the same set of principles of individual natural rights flowed from 1776, to Mason's objections to Madison's document 12 years later.

The proximate cause of Mason's objections to Madison's document is not the absence of a Bill of Rights.

The reason for Mason's objections is that Madison's document left out the part about "all power derived from the consent of the governed," and replaced that principle with the moral superiority of the ruling class to make political decisions on behalf of common citizens.

Driesbach notes that Mason also included a number of rights which Madison belatedly included in Madison's Bill of Rights, in 1791.

In particular, Mason listed rights of those accused of capital or criminal offenses. These rights included trial by an impartial jury, the right of the accused to be confronted by witnesses and/or accusers, that no part of a person's property can be taken from him, or applied to public use, without the consent of himself, or his legal representatives and the right to be free from excessive bail and fines, as well as from cruel and unusual punishments.

We argue that after the election of 2020, that the Bill of Rights, especially the right of unreasonable search and seizure, are routinely evaded by the agents of the deep state, in order for the agents to prosecute their political enemies.

Mason's intent in drafting the Virginia Constitution was to create a framework of government that would allow citizens the freedom to pursue their individual interests, while cooperating with other citizens in forming laws, in a state sovereignty participatory government.

According to Helen Hill, the goal of Mason's draft constitution was,

"…to create a political framework within which every citizen should be free to exercise the rights which he, as an individual, was competent to exercise and within which the government should secure to the citizens the rights which they were incapable of maintaining in their individual capacities…States rights to Mason was not the negative slogan of jealous particularism: it was rather the positive slogan of jealous participation…Mason saw a division of public functions among citizens, states, and the federal government which would give content to the general statements of the Bill of Rights." (Hill, Helen, George Mason: Constitutionalist, Peter Smith Edition, 1966.).

Hill outlined the major features of Mason's draft constitution. She writes,

"Mason's constitution established separate executive, and judicial departments, and a bicameral general assembly. The lower house to consist of two representatives from each county chosen annually from freeholders upwards of twenty-four years of age, such representatives to be resident in the county for at least a year and possessed of landed estates of at least $1,000 value. For election to the upper house, the state was to be divided into twenty-four districts, in each of whose constituent counties twelve subelectors would be chosen from resident freeholders with estates of at least £500 value; These subelectors would then choose one member for the twenty-four-member upper house from resident freeholders. Legislation originated in a popularly elected lower house. Except for money bills, the upper house could accept, reject, or amend any bill but it could only vote tax and appropriations bills up or down, by a joint ballot, a governor, and the attorney general, were chosen annually by joint ballot of both Houses. The governor could serve three consecutive one-year terms and was ineligible to hold the office for three years. Two councillors [on the 8-member Council of State] were replaced every three years and would be ineligible to serve on the council for the next three years. The governor, with the advice of the council, could appoint militia officers and justices of the peace. Most other local official were appointed by the governor and the council upon nomination. All "officers of government" could be impeached "for maladministration or corruption" by the lower house and tried before a summit. Commissions, writs, and indictments would be made in the name of the "commonwealth," nomenclature taken from John Locke that to signify the supremacy of the legislature."

Hill emphasizes the essential function of the Virginia Council of State, to act as a check against the power of a rogue governor.

Mason never abandoned his insistence that Madison's rules were deliberately weak because Madison adamantly rejected the idea of a check against a rogue President.

Mason believed that each state had a unique social culture and political system that the Articles of Confederation preserved. Mason attempted to transfer the state sovereignty framework from the Articles to Madison's document, prior to the end of the Convention, when Mason realized that Madison's rules would end in a centralized aristocratic tyranny.

According to John Kaminsky and Richard Leffler, Mason believed that in each state,

"The laws and customs of the several stats are very diverse and in some opposite....composed of such heterogenous and discordant principles as would constantly be contending with each other...The confidence the people have in their rulers arises in a free republic from them knowing them ...the consequence [of the centralized government] will be by establishing an armed force to execute the law at the point of a bayonet." (Kaminsky, John and Leffler, Richard, Federalists and Antifederalists: The Debate Over the Ratification of the Constitution, Madison House, 1998.)

Mason's arguments about preserving the framework of state sovereignty was based upon his understanding of Montesquieu's principles of a small geographical republic.

Mason stated,

"In so extensive a republic the great officers of government would soon become above the control of the people and abuse their power to the purpose of aggrandizing themselves and oppressing the people… I fear the thirst for power will prevail to oppress the people…I always fear for the rights of the people… [in the] aristocratic nature of the Senate, once Senators get in office it is feared they might be reelected perpetually, for life." (Kaminsky, and Leffler, 1998.).

In arguing against Mason's state sovereignty principles, in Federalist #10, Madison distorted and subverted Montesquieu's principles about an extended republic

In Federalist # 10 Madison argued,

"The other point of difference [between a republic and democracy], is the greater number of citizens and extent of territory which may be brought within the compass of republican than of democratic government; and it is this circumstance principally which renders *factious* combinations less to be dreaded in the former than in the latter."

The key to understanding Madison's distortion of Montesquieu's principles is in Madison's continued imaginary red-herring use of the term "faction."

Common citizens in America were not organized into a political faction. The natural aristocracy was an organized financial faction.

Madison distorted Montesquieu's principles of a republic by arguing that bigger districts were actually better than smaller ones because they afforded a wider pool of persons from whom the most capable representatives could be drawn.

As Jacob T. Levy points out, Madison's logic of his extended republic is based upon his concept of competing social class factions, which existed in England.

Madison stated in Federalist #10, regarding the multitude of competing factions,

"The more extended the republic the greater difficulty in assembling a tyrannical majority faction." (Levy, Jacob T., Beyond Publius: Montesquieu, Liberal Republicanism and the Small-Republic Thesis, JSTOR, 2006.)

The tyrannical majority faction was the imaginary common citizen faction. Madison falsely projected his fear that the common citizens would form a tyrannical majority faction that would deprive the natural aristocracy of their unelected and unwarranted privileges.

Madison's extended republic ensured that the common citizens would never form a social class consciousness of their own financial interests that may compete with the existing well-organized ruling class faction.

Levy cites Jefferson as pointing out the logical flaw in Madison's rules regarding the extended republic.

"Large republics could better protect freedom than a small one, but only if, and in part, because of it was organized with both separation of powers and federalism. [state sovereignty] When all government, domestic and foreign, in little as in great things, shall be drawn to Washington as the center of all power, it will render powerless the checks and balances provided one government on another, and will become as venal and oppressive as the government from which we separated."

The main effect of Madison's extended republic was to create permanent barriers to the common citizens ever developing a coherent social class ideology, because when the geographically dispersed representatives arrive in Washington, they engage in the ideology of shared plunder, not the defense of individual liberty.

Kaminsky and Leffler cite Cato's criticism of Madison's logic of the extended republic.

"[The representatives from the extended republic will be] composed of interests opposite and dissimilar in their nature, and [the government] will in its exercise emphatically be like a house divided against itself by indispensibly placing trust in the hands of individuals whose ambitions for power and agrandisement will oppress and grind you." [after they get to Washington]. (1998.).

As Mason correctly predicted, Madison's rules would,

"Become an elective Monarchy…[the natural aristocracy] would suffer under an equal application [of the law] in which office holders are responsible."

Mason's argument about state sovereignty was based upon his understanding that the corrupt British social class framework of government would only work in a centralized tyranny, not in a decentralized state-sovereignty framework of government.

As Mason stated in his letter to New York Governor Clinton, during the Virginia ratifying convention of 1788,

Mason wrote,

"The first [principle]is a virtual quotation from Article II of the Articles of Confederation, securing each state's "sovereignty, freedom and independence, and every Power Jurisdiction and Right, which is not by this Constitution *expressly* delegated to the Congress of the United States."

The term "expressly delegated" by the states to the central government is the seminal principle of Mason's state sovereignty framework of government.

Madison eliminated the term "expressly delegated" from his rendition of Article 10, in his Bill of Rights of 1791, leaving the central government with unlimited implied powers over both states and citizens.

Chapter 3. Mason's Lifetime Crusade Against the Corruption and Tyranny Inherent in the British Mixed Social Class Conflict Model.

Many historical accounts of Mason's life emphasize that he did not sign the draft Constitution on September 17, 1787, because it did not contain a Bill of Rights.

We argue that the absence of a bill of rights is a subordinate cause of his refusal to sign the document.

The predominant cause of Mason's refusal to sign the document was his conviction that Madison's document replicated the corrupt tyranny of the British social class conflict model of government.

Long before he refused to sign Madison's document, Mason had warned that the British social class conflict model was inherently, and systemically, corrupt.

The absence of a Bill of Rights was just one of Mason's many objections to Madison's replication of the British social class conflict model that elevated the financial and political interests of Madison's so-called natural aristocracy over the interests of common citizens, just as the British model elevated the interests of the British

House of Lords over the interests of British common citizens.

Mason's ancestor, Robert C. Mason, summarized some of the other main objections to the Constitution that George Mason had expressed to members of his family.

"It did not abolish slavery or make preparation for its gradual extinction, it did not clearly define the sovereign rights of the states, or positively declare the fundamental constitutional prerogatives of the federal government. It left the door open for the possibility of a civil war, and it made possible the creeping in of arbitrary power which in a republic, no less than in a monarchy, is ever prone to usurp place and authority." (George Mason of Virginia, Oscar Aurlius Morgner, 1919.).

It was towards the end of the convention in August of 1787, that Mason realized that what Madison had in mind was to make the proposed U. S. Senate function like the British House of Lords, and to make the office of the U. S. President function like the British king, but without the King's Council.

The delayed realization by Mason about Madison's plan was primarily because a small committee of detail had not shared the final version of the draft document about the function of the President with the other delegates.

By the time Mason and the other delegates finally saw the Brearly Committee's last unfinished draft, on September 4, 1787, there was no time left in the convention for Mason to change the draft in the open debate, because the other delegates would not second, or refused to vote, on Mason's motions.

However, even after September 4, the final document continued to be changed and modified, in secret, up until the night of September 16, 1787, when Madison inserted the revised Fugitive Slave clause, which had been deleted in the previous open debates, in late August.

The first time Mason was able to see all of the changes made by Madison was on the morning of September 17, 1787.

William G. Hyland, Jr. writes that at the end of the Convention,

"Mason was convinced that the fundamental principles of the Revolution stood in jeopardy." (Hyland, William G., George Mason: The Founding Father Who Gave Us The Bill of Rights, Regnery History, 2019.).

Hyland notes that towards the end of the Convention, Mason realized that,

"What is being proposed…was the creation of a central government that looks suspiciously to them just like the British government that they had been fighting against…the political system that Mason favored would ensure that the exercise of arbitrary, excessive and dictatorial power would be prevented…what Mason feared most in a central government was too powerful an executive… the president could use his patronage to corrupt Congress…the government will degenerate into a monarchy."

Mason contrasted the British mixed social class conflict model of government with the proposed framework of Madison's government.

Mason argued that in the British model, the House of Lords could not dominate the King, unlike in Madison, where the President [surrogate king] and Senate were from the same social class natural aristocracy.

Mason reasoned that, if Madison was intent on replicating the British model of government, then the President should have a Council of State to check the power of a rogue President.

Brent Tarter writes,

"In the opinion of Mason, imperfections in the structure of the British government had undermined the once sound principles of the [unwritten] British constitution and allowed corruption to disrupt or destroy the well-balanced system that mixed the three estates of society [royalty, nobility and commons] in a government of interlocking executive, legislative and judicial institutions." (Tarter, Brent, George Mason and the Conservation of Liberty, The Virginia Magazine of History and Biography, July 1991.).

Mason had written, in the Fairfax Resolves, that,

"The most important and valuable part of the British Constitution, upon which its very existence depends, is, the fundamental principle of the people being governed by no laws to which they have not given their consent by Representatives freely chosen by themselves, who are affected by the laws they enact equally with their constituents, to whom they are accountable, and whose burthens they [the elected representatives] share, in which consists the safety and happiness of the community; for if this part of the [British] Constitution was taken away or materially altered the government must degenerate either into an absolute and despotic monarchy, or a tyrannical aristocracy, and the freedom of the people be annihilated."

During the Convention, in the debates about the power of the President, in late August, Mason argued,

"It seems as if it were taken for granted that all offices will be filled by the Executive, while I think many will remain in the gift of the legislature. In either case it is necessary to shut the door against corruption. If otherwise, they [the Senate] may make or multiply places in order to fill them. . . . We must, in the present system remove the temptation [of corruption]. I admire many parts of the British constitution and government, but I detest their corruption. Why has the power of the crown increased, so remarkably increased, the last century?"

Gordon Wood observed that,

"Mason feared corruption at any level of government more than he feared the consolidation of power in a national government....The thirst of power will prevail to oppress the people. Bribery and corruption will be practiced in America more than in England." (Wood, Gordon, The Making of the Constitution, Baylor University Press, 1987.).

David Siemers noted that, on September 15, 1787, the last day of open debate at the Convention, Mason stated,

"The plan of amendments is exceptionable and dangerous. As the proposing of amendments in both modes to depend in the first immediately and in the second ultimately on Congress, no amendments of the proper kind would ever be obtained by the people, if the Government should become oppressive, as he verily believed would be the case." (Siemers, David J., The Antifederalists: Men of Great Faith and Forbearance, Rowman & Littlefield Publishers, 2003.).

At the very end of the Convention, Mason repeatedly warned the other delegates that Madison's rules would lead to a corrupt centralized elite tyranny.

From Madison's notes:

Mr. RANDOLPH. We have in some revolutions of this plan made a bold stroke for Monarchy. We are now doing the same for an aristocracy. He dwelt on the tendency of such an influence in the Senate over the election of the President in addition to its other powers, to convert that body into a real & dangerous Aristocracy.

Col: MASON. As the mode of appointment is now regulated, he could not forbear expressing his opinion that it is utterly inadmissible. He would prefer the Government of Prussia to one which will put all power into the hands of seven or eight men, and fix an Aristocracy worse than absolute monarchy. The words "and of their giving their votes" being inserted on motion for that purpose, after the words "The Legislature may determine the time of chusing and assembling the electors."

September 7. Col: MASON said that in rejecting a Council to the President we were about to try an experiment on which the most despotic Governments had never ventured. The Grand Signor himself had his Divan. He moved to postpone the consideration of the clause in order to take up the following:

"That it be an instruction to the Committee of the States to prepare a clause or clauses for establishing an Executive Council, as a Council of State, for the President of the U. States, to consist of six members, two of which from the Eastern, two from the middle, and two from the Southern States, with a Rotation and duration of office similar to those of the Senate; such Council to be appointed by the Legislature or by the Senate."

September 8. A Committee was then appointed by Ballot to revise the stile of and arrange the articles which had been agreed to by the House. The committee consisted of Mr. Johnson, Mr. Hamilton, Mr. Govr. Morris, Mr.Madison and Mr. King.

September 15. [the last day of open debate] Col: MASON. 2ded. & followed Mr. Randolph in animadversions on the dangerous power and structure of the Government, concluding that it would end either in monarchy, or a tyrannical aristocracy; which, he was in doubt, but one or other, he was sure. This Constitution had been formed without the knowledge or idea of the people. A second Convention will know more of the sense of the people, and be able to provide a system more consonant to it. It was improper to say to the people, take this or nothing.

Mason's language for describing Madison's scheme, on September 15, "take this or nothing," went directly to the heart of Madison's duplicity in creating his constitution, without providing citizens an alternative form of government, even the most limited choice between Madison's document and the Articles of Confederation.

The entire body of delegates, prior to the appointment of the Committee on Style, on September 8, had not reached agreement or debated the powers of the Presidency, because the Brearly Committee of September 4, did not include the finished clauses about the powers of the Presidency.

The Committee on Style never released the final clauses of Article II, on the Presidency to the delegates, before they voted on them, on the final day of open debate, on September 15.

Mason stated that,

"Considering the powers of the President & those of the Senate, if a coalition should be established between these two branches, they will be able to subvert the Constitution."

As Mason's fellow natural rights compatriot, Brutus wrote,

"The judiciary under this system will have a power which is above the legislative, and which indeed transcends any power before given to a judicial by any free government under heaven."

In The Framers Coup, Michael Klarman, (2016), noted the statement of another anti-federalist,

"The Georgia antifederalist stated that the constitution paves the way for an aristocratical government whereby about 70 nabobs would lord over 3 million citizens as slaves. In "rule by the wealthy."

Melancton Smith, another natural rights delegate to the convention, wrote that,

"The Constitution is radically defective. It vests in Congress great and uncountroulable powers that it will use to annihilate all the state governments, and reduce this country to one single government."

Smith warned that instead of creating a balance of power, Madison's constitution would combine ruling class legislative power with judicial power that would eventually destroy the local and state governments.

He stated that the Supreme Court would interpret the Constitution according to the justices', "spirit and reason, [ruling class ideology] and they would mold the government into any shape they please."

As noted by Brutus, a natural rights proponent, during the ratification debates,

"The framers of this constitution appear to have followed that of the British, in rendering the judges independent, by granting them their offices during good behaviour, without following the constitution of England, in instituting a tribunal in which their errors may be corrected; [by the King] and without adverting to this, that the judicial under this system have a power which is above the legislative, and which indeed transcends any power before given to a judicial by any free government under heaven."

Brutus reiterated this sentiment. He wrote,

"The costs of [legal representation] in the supreme court will be so great, as to put it out of the reach of the poor and middling class of citizens to contest a suit in it."

The judicial system, in other words, was designed from the get-go, to be the exclusive province of the wealthy elite, who had the money to pursue justice, and who would, subsequently, use that legal power to deprive common citizens of their property, as in the debt-lien system applied against common farmers, in the 1880s.

Madison's version of the British mixed system left out the part about the King and his Council, the power of the King to remove judges, and omitted the part about the British multi-party parliamentary system, based upon the financial conflict between British social classes.

As Forrest McDonald explains,

"In the English system each branch of government represented people whose status was inherited...In the United States, there was no hereditary status...therefore [Madison's] the English model was inappropriate...[The British] constitution separated the people from government in two ways: some officials were chosen directly [by the aristocracy]; there was also the time barrier…there was no way for the people could express their will directly and immediately." (McDonald. Forrest, A Constitutional History of the United States. Franklin Watts, 1982.).

The British mixed system does not function for obtaining justice without the King, acting as the final authority of what actions constitute justice, and it does not function unless the separation of power is based upon the competition between social classes.

Philanthropos wrote, Madison's constitution would allow,

"The people are to be fleeced, and the public business neglected. From despotism and tyranny, good Lord deliver us."

Both Madison and Hamilton knew exactly what the role of corruption would be in Madison's constitution for maintaining elite control over economic and banking policy.

Corruption, also known as shared plunder, was the glue that held Madison's economic system together.

Hamilton stated, in his 1792 dinner with Jefferson that,

"Purge the Government of its corruption and give to its popular branch equality of representation and it would become an impracticable government."

Corruption and investment speculation were tied together, in Madison's rules, by the ability of the elite to manipulate the nation's money supply to suit their own social class interests.

The motive behind Hamilton's promotion of corruption in the financial system was to preserve the benefits of speculation in the land transactions by members of the natural aristocracy.

In "Information, Markets, and Corruption: Transcontinental Railroads in the Gilded Age, Richard White describes how Madison's rules facilitated extensive and pervasive corruption during the American Gilded Age.

He writes,

"Corruption is a species of fraud that involves violation of public or private trust. A covenant of some sort, either implied or explicit, [Jefferson's promise of liberty] is violated. Corruption involves betrayal, often of a third party. The corrupt buy or sell what was not supposed to be for sale, a vote, for example, or public property. They turn to personal advantage and their legal status as trustees of persons or property. Or they grant only to a privileged few what is purportedly available to all or available only through open and fair competition." (The Journal of American History, June 2003.).

White is describing Madison's more perfect union of "Get-Rich-Quick," for the privileged few of Madison's natural aristocracy.

Madison's constitution was about governance of special interest corruption among factions, not about democratic citizen participation in government.

Madison's more perfect union was not a union of states, nor a union between common citizens and the new government.

Madison's more perfect union was a compact between the natural aristocracy and the agencies of government, held together by the cultural value of shared plunder.

Madison used the British mixed government as his model of American society, and recreated a version of the British social class society in America, where the American natural aristocracy had their own branch of government, and were insulated from the influence of common citizens.

Madison's rules created the legal framework for elite rule, and Hamilton then added the financial system that benefitted the plutocracy as a result of money supply and interest rate manipulation.

As Goodwyn notes, in The Populist Moment,

"The ultimate monopoly was the money trust, a banking system of private plunder anchored in a metallic currency and assured of political power because it [Ruling Class] owned both sound money parties...The destruction of the cooperatives by the banks was a decisive blow, for it weakened the interior structure of [the Agrarian] democracy." (Goodwyn, Lawrence, The Populist Moment: A Short History of the Agrarian Revolt in America, Oxford University Press, 1978.).

In Mason's and Jefferson's version of the American Dream, common citizens share social cultural values of equal opportunity for economic prosperity, which tends to bind citizens to voluntarily obey the rule of law.

Mason's concept of government was about state sovereignty and citizen democracy that reduced the unelected power of the natural aristocracy to exploit common citizens.

The origin of the conflict between two versions of the American history lies in how the story of American history is told by scholars and academics, who combine and conflate two distinct, and separate historical events [1776 and 1787] at the beginning of the American nation.

The two distinct and separate events are combined by academic historians into a historical myth that there was only one consolidated event, called "the founding."

In the telling of that national narrative myth, Mason did not sign Madison's document because it did not contain a Bill of Rights.

Telling the myth about Mason's reasons for not signing the Constitution allows the scholarly community to cite Jefferson's Declaration, and not Mason's Declaration of Rights, on the principles of equality, as evidence that Madison's constitution is not immoral, it is simply evolving to become a "more perfect union."

We offer an alternative explanation of the immorality of Madison's constitution that features the disenfranchisement of the consent of the governed of common citizens, in a transfer of sovereignty from states to a consolidated tyrannical central government.

Madison's perspective of the two competing social classes in America was half right.

The natural aristocracy had already formed themselves into a coherent social class, which functioned as a political party during the Convention.

Mason conducted a life-long battle against the corruption of Madison's British mixed government model because he knew, from his own personal family perspective, as a Virginia aristocrat, how the British system of corruption worked.

The British system of corruption was already working for the American ruling class, in 1787, when Madison called the Convention to organize.

The process and procedures for selecting delegates to attend the Convention was corrupt.

As noted by Federal Farmer,

Pennsylavania appointed principally those men who are esteemed aristocratical...Ten other states appointed men principally connected with commerce and the judicial department. In the nature of things, nine times in ten, men of elevated classes in the community only can be chosen—Connecticut, for instance, will have five representatives—not one man in a hundred of those who form the democratic branch in the state legislature, will on a fair computation, be one of the five—The people of this country, in one sense, may all be democratic; but if we make the proper distinction between the few men of wealth and abilities, and consider them, as we ought, as the natural aristocracy of the country, and the great body of the people, the middle and lower classes, as the democracy; this federal representative branch will have but very little democracy in it, even this small representation is not secured on proper principles. . ." (Kaminsky John, and Leffler, Richard, ed., Federalists and Antifederalists: The Debate Over the Ratification of the Constitution, Madison House, 1998.).

Kaminsky and Leffler cite the article by Centinel about the secret political work by the natural aristocracy to overthrow the Articles of Confederation.

Centinel writes,

In many of the states, particularly in this and the northern states, there are aristocratic junto's of the well-born few, who had been zealously endeavouring since the establishment of their [state] constitutions, to humble that offensive upstart, equal liberty; but all their efforts were un-availing, the ill-bred churl [common citizens] obstinately kept his assumed station… A comparison of the authority under which the convention acted, and their form of government will show that they have despised their delegated power, [to amend the Articles of Confederation] and assumed sovereignty; that they have entirely annihilated the old confederation, and the particular governments of the several states, and instead thereof have established one general government that is to pervade the union; constituted on the most unequal principles, destitute of accountability to its constituents, and as despotic in its nature, as the Venetian aristocracy; a government that will give full scope to the magnificent designs of the well-born; a government where tyranny May glut its vengeance on the low-born, unchecked by an odious bill of rights: as has been fully illustrated in my two preceding numbers."

Federal Farmer provided details of the tiny minority of American elites who conspired to overthrow the Articles of Confederation in order to implement their corrupt British form of government.

Federal Farmer's insights into the coherent social class ideology of the natural aristocracy documents their existing social class power to overthrow the government.

Federal Farmer wrote,

In my idea of our natural aristocracy in the United States, I include about four or five thousand men; and among these I reckon those who have been placed in the offices of governors, of members of Congress, and state senators generally, in the principal officers of Congress, of the army and militia, the superior judges, the most eminent professional men, &c. and men of large property*—the other. persons and orders in the community form the natural democracy; this includes in general the yeomanry, the subordinate officers, civil and military, the fishermen, mechanics and traders, many of the merchants and professional men. It is easy to perceive that men of these two classes, the aristocratical, and democratical, with views equally honest, have sentiments widely different, especially respecting public and private expences, salaries, taxes, &c. Men of the first class associate more extensively, have a high sense of honor, possess abilities, ambition, and general knowledge: men of the second class are not so much used to combining great objects; they possess less ambition, and a larger share of honesty: their dependence is principally on middling and small estates, industrious pursuits, and hard labour, while that of the former is principally on the emoluments of large estates, and of the chief offices of government. Not only the efforts of these two great parties are to be balanced, but other interests and parties also, which do not always oppress each other merely for want of power, and for fear of the consequences; though they, in fact, mutually depend on each other; yet such are their general views, that the merchants alone would never fail to make laws favourable to themselves and oppressive to the farmers, &c. the farmers alone would act on like principles; the former would tax the land, the latter, the trade. The manufacturers are often disposed to contend for monopolies, buyers make every exertion to lower prices, and sellers to raise them; men who live by fees and salaries endeavour to raise them, and the part of the people who pay them, endeavour to lower them; the public creditors to augment the taxes, and the people at large to lessen them."

Melancton Smith, of New York, wrote in 1788, that the common citizens would not have a fair chance to prosper under Madison's rules.

Smith wrote,

"This will be a government of oppression. I am convinced that this government is so constituted, that the representatives will generally be composed of the first class in the community, which I shall distinguish by the name of the natural aristocracy of the country. I do not mean to give offence by using this term. I am sensible this idea is treated by many gentlemen as chimerical. I shall be asked what is meant by the natural aristocracy, and told that no such distinction of classes of men exists among us. [all in this together]. It is true it is our singular felicity, that we have no legal or hereditary distinctions of this kind; but still there are real differences: Every society naturally divides itself into classes. The author of nature has bestowed on some greater capacities than on others—birth, education, talents and wealth, create distinctions among men as visible and of as much influence as titles, stars and garters. In every society, men of this class will command a superior degree of respect—and if the government is so constituted as to admit but few to exercise the powers of it, it will, according to the natural course of 'things, be in their hands. Men in the middling class, who are qualified as representatives, will not be so anxious to be chosen as those of the first. When the number is so small the office will be highly elevated and distinguished—the style in which the members live will probably be high—

circumstances of this kind, will render the place of a representative not a desirable one to sensible, substantial men, who have been used, to walk in the plain and frugal paths of life."

Smith continues his article by describing Madison's flawed rendition of the "extended republic."

Smith writes,

Besides, the influence of the great [ruling class] will generally enable them to succeed in elections—it will be difficult to combine a district of country containing 30 or 40,000 inhabitants, frame your election laws as you please, in any one character; unless it be in one of conspicuous military civil, or legal talents. [ruling class]. The great easily form associations; the poor and middling class form them with difficulty If the elections be by plurality, as probably will be the case in this state, it is almost certain, none but the great will be chosen—for they easily unite their interests—The common people will divide, and their divisions will be promoted by the others. There will be scarcely a chance of their uniting, in any other but some great man, unless in some popular demagogue, who will probably be destitute of principle. A substantial yeoman of sense and discernment, will hardly ever be chosen. From these remarks it appears that the government will fall into the hands of the few and the great. This will be a government of oppression."

The terms and phrases used by Smith, that the government will be one of oppression is the same language used by Mason to describe Madison's rules.

Madison admits, during the debates in the Convention that the American common citizens have not yet formed themselves into a coherent social class, like the common citizens in Europe.

Madison anticipates that the common citizens will eventually form themselves into a social class with a coherent middle class ideology, and that his rules are designed to thwart that future circumstance.

From Farrand Records, vol. 1, pp. 421-423.

"Madison said: The three principle classes. into which our citizens are divisible, were the landed, the commercial, & the manufacturing. The 3rd, class bears as yet a small proportion to the first. Their number however will daily increase. We see in the populous Countries in Europe what we shall be hereafter...in process of time, when we approximate to the kingdoms of Europe; when the number of landholders shall be comparatively small, through the various means of trade and manufactures, an not the landed interest be overbalanced in future elections, and unless provided against, what will become of your government? In England, if elections were open to all classes of people, the property of the landed proprietors would be insecure. An agrarian law would soon take place. If these observations be just, our government ought to secure the permanent threats of the country against innovation. [common citizens]. Landholders ought to have a share of the government to support these invaluable interests and to balance and check the other. They ought to be so constituted as to protect the minority of the population against the majority. The senate, therefore, ought to be this body; In order to answer these purposes, they ought to have permanency and stability. Those have been the propositions; but my opinion is, the longer they continue in in office, the better will these views be answered. (Slonim, Shlomo, Framers' Construction/Beardian Deconstruction, Essays on the Constitutional Design of 1787, Peter Lanf Publishing, 2001.).

From Farrand's Records, vol. 1, pp. 430-431.

"The delegates frequently referred to the Senate as the "aristocratic "body in the legislature, Deigned to restrain or balance the turbulent lower or "democratic" house. The Senate was meant to represent and protect "wealth," there was even the suggestion that membership therein be conditional on the ownership of considerable property. The proposal was rejected, as was a suggestion that legislators not be paid a salary, to encourage only the wealthy to submit their names as candidates."

Farrand notes that Charles Pinckney, a delegate from South Carolina, also assumed that the as-yet-created American common citizen ideology would eventually replicate the social class structure of England, which would threaten the existing social class ideology of the ruling class.

Pinckney is quoted, during the Convention,

"The United States is divided into three different classes: (1) professional men, (2) commercial: men, and (3) "The landed interest, the owners and cultivators are the, and ought ever to be the governing spring in the system over the commercial class. Pinckney said: "If that commercial policy [favoring the landed interests] is pursued, conceive it to be the true one, the merchants of this Country will not for a considerable time have much: weight in the political scale."

Slonin quotes Gouverneur Morris, an aristocrat delegate from New York, who strangely represented Pennsylvania, as almost giddy at the thought of oppressing the common citizens.

Slonin quotes Morris,

"The Rich will strive to establish their dominion and enslave the rest. They always did. They always will. The proper security agst. them is to form them into a separate interest. The two forces will then controul each other. Let the rich mix with the poor and in a Commercial Country, they will establish an Oligarchy.. . By thus combining & setting, apart, the aristocratic interest, the popular interest will be combined agst. it. There will be a mutual check and mutual security [for the ruling class]. (Slonim, 2001.).

Madison, like the 38 other delegates at the Convention, knew they had conducted their deliberations in secret, and also knew that the rules were permanently stacked against the financial interests of the common citizens.

Mason also knew this fact.

David Stewart, in The Summer of 1787: The Men Who Invented the Constitution, quoted Madison's letter to Jefferson, written on the last day of the Convention.

"Madison wrote nervously about the nation beyond the East Room of the State House. "Nothing," he assured Jefferson,"can exceed the universal anxiety for the event of the meeting here. Reports and conjectures abound concerning the nature of the plan which is to be proposed."…Madison acknowledged to Jefferson that the public was "certainly in the dark" as to the new Constitution, but he was more troubled that the [38 delegates to the] Convention [are] equally in the dark as to the reception which may be given to it. Would it be acclaimed or reviled? Though "certain characters [Mason]will wage war against any reform," Madison hoped Americans would accept "anything that promises stability to the public councils and security to private rights." Still, he added, "if the present moment be lost, it is hard to say what may be our fate [refers to the fate of the natural aristocracy using the royal "we." (Simon & Schuster. 2007.).

In violation of both Locke's and Mason's image of citizens agreeing to a voluntary transfer of their rights to government in order to more fully secure their natural rights, the common citizens, in 1787, lost their natural rights, without gaining the benefits of liberty, in the exchange with Madison.

The citizens were never given a chance to vote to ratify the transfer of sovereignty and never agreed upon the establishment of Madison's plutocracy.

Mason lost his life-long battle against the corruption inherent in the British social class conflict model, and the victors, who wrote the American historical narrative myth, punished the reputation of Mason, by cancelling the accurate history of his egalitarian principles in the Virginia Declaration of Rights and his constitutional framework of liberty in the Virginia Constitution.

Chapter 4. Shays' Rebellion and Madison's War Against State-Issued Paper Money.

Many scholarly accounts of the history surrounding the events leading up to the Constitutional Convention of 1787 emphasize a set of factors related to the inadequacy of the Articles of Confederation.

For example, Jeff Broadwater cites the list of factors surrounding the reasons for calling the Convention provided by Forrest McDonald. (George Mason: The Forgotten Founder, 2006.).

McDonald identified 4 broad factors that precipitated Madison's calling of the convention:

- Landless states jealous of neighbors with territorial claims in the West.
- Commercial states anxious to protect their carrying trade.
- Planters seeking to protect agricultural exports and in S. C. and in Georgia, the foreign slave trade.
- Public creditors and investors who were concerned about the solvency of the central government.

The national narrative myth about the reasons for calling the Convention are built around these ephemeral issues, and do not address the primary financial factors surrounding Madison's convening of the Convention.

The national narrative myth begins in 1787, not in 1775, and the scholarly community adopts the perspective of the natural aristocracy that the Articles of Confederation were defective, beyond repair.

It is essential for promoting the national narrative myth that the factors surrounding the Convention do not identify social class conflict in the American society, as the reason for convening the Convention.

According to the myth, there was only one founding event, by the 38 virtuous and selfless founding fathers, who signed the document on September 17, 1787, under the pretense of "We, the people."

This unified national narrative perspective of the historians about the founding is essential to promoting the subsequent obscurity of George Mason's reputation as a founding father because Mason was the only delegate to address the social class conflict surrounding Madison's Convention.

Robert Hoffert, in The Politics of Tension, describes the national narrative myth as "a homogenized" account of the events surrounding the calling of the Convention.

Hoffert writes,

"By starting their national story in 1787, American (historians) schooled themselves on a homogenized account of their [American] political identity." (A Politics of Tensions: The Articles of Confederation and American Political Ideas, University Press of Colorado 1992.).

The authentic American political identity emerged on the field of battle, in 1775, not 1787.

In the aftermath of Lexington and Concord, in April of 1775, America's patriot founders began meeting to discuss what form of government would replace the British monarchy.

Their deliberations culminated in the creation of the Articles of Confederation, adopted by all 13 states in 1781.

We argue that those early discussions were the beginning of the shared cultural value of American liberty, held by all patriots.

The term used by Patriots to describe that common value was the "Spirit of '76."

In addition to the discussions about the form of government, the patriots shared a common experience of fighting a war with Great Britain.

The war with King George forged a national identity among the patriot soldiers, similar to the shared consciousness of the soldiers who fought in the Civil War, and later, in both World Wars, and the War in Viet Nam.

The soldiers who returned home after those wars shared a collective consciousness about what it meant to be an American.

As written by Gordon Wood, in The Radicalism of the American Revolution,

"To be an American could not be a matter of blood; it had to be a matter of common belief and behavior. And the source of that common belief and behavior was the American Revolution: it was the revolution and only the Revolution that made them one people." (Wood, Gordon, The Radicalism of the American Revolution, Vintage, 1993.).

The point Wood is making is that the first American Revolution forged a common set of national cultural and social values that bound all citizens together into a shared national mission of liberty.

C. Bradley Thompson, in his book, America's Revolutionary Mind, describes the constellation of common beliefs held by anti-federalists, as the "American Moral Philosophy," and cites Locke's admonition that citizens who adhere to the American civic virtue do not undermine the liberty of other citizens. (Thompson, C. Bradley, America's Revolutionary Mind: A Moral History of the American Revolution and the Declaration That Defined It, Encounter Books, 2019.).

Thompson wrote,

"Locke's fundamental law of nature (i.e., to follow right reason) issues two commands: first, each and, every man should pursue his rational, long-term self-interest; and, second, "No one ought to harm another in his life, health, liberty, or possessions."

John Locke had written that shared cultural values, and shared common social experiences, were the necessary precursor conditions for forming a new government, when the citizens left the state of nature.

George Mason and Thomas Jefferson relied upon this shared national identity of individual liberty, when they wrote their respective documents on individual liberty and rights of common citizens, in 1776.

In The Antifederalists: Men of Great Faith and Forbearance, David J. Siemers, summarizes Mason's arguments against ratification.

Siemers noted that on September 15, 1787, the last day of open public debate at the convention, Mason stated,

"The plan of amendments is exceptionable and dangerous. As the proposing of amendments in both modes to depend in the first immediately and in the second ultimately on Congress, no amendments of the proper kind would ever be obtained by the people, if the Government should become oppressive, as he verily believed would be the case."

The mistake in judgment made by George Mason about the convening of the Convention was that he assumed that Madison also shared this cultural value of individual freedom.

In 1787, there were not any commonly-shared cultural values between George Mason's Spirit of '76, and James Madison's cultural value of elite shared plunder.

Mason's concept of equal liberty leads to one version of the American Dream of equal economic opportunity.

The shared cultural values of economic and political equality are essential for the operation of a democratic republic because the values establish the condition for voluntary citizen allegiance to obey the rule of law.

Brian Balogh, in A Government Out of Sight: The Mystery of National Authority in Nineteenth-Century America, explained the contrast between the Mason/Jefferson concept of the American Dream and Madison's American Dream,

"Jefferson forged a historical interpretation that pitted the interests of the people, expressed through the ballot box against the will of a small elite. Jefferson's "empire of liberty" thus knit Americans together across a vast expanse by bonds of affection reinforced by material interest." (Cambridge University Press, 2009.).

In the Jefferson version of the American Dream, Balogh writes,

"Jefferson envisioned a republic populated by independent farmers tied to their country and wedded to its liberty and interests by the most lasting bands… a nation of one heart and one mind. The proponents of the Dream argued that enterprising citizens could create value, value that the larger community would ultimately share. Wealth…produced more wealth in the form of capital."

Balogh's statement about wealth creating more wealth echoes Adam Smith, in The Wealth of Nations.

Madison's and Hamilton's version of the Dream was based upon the application of Hamilton's "real bills" doctrine, that stated that the corruption surrounding speculative investments of the ruling class would always lead to real economic growth.

Madison and Hamilton's version of the American Dream leads to a cultural value of shared plunder of financial and economic assets by the natural aristocracy.

The distribution of income and wealth from ruling class plunder is not distributed widely, to all social classes, through the income and employment multipliers of a free competitive market.

In Madison's culture of shared plunder, obedience to the rule of law is enforced by Leviathan, which is currently in the hands of Democrat Marxists.

We argue that Madison replaced the shared cultural value of the "Spirit of '76, with the cultural value of ruling class shared plunder, obtained by the elites in the political corruption of the spoils system, after the Constitution had been implemented.

When George Mason realized what Madison intended, on the last day of the Convention, he wrote his document on his objections to Madison's document, ending with his prediction of a ruling class aristocracy.

His objections were made in the historical context that Madison's rules were violating the spirit of the Revolution, in other words, "The Spirit of '76."

The Articles of Confederation were not defective, from the perspective of common citizens and soldiers who fought in the Revolution. The Articles defined what it meant to be an American citizen in a state-sovereignty constitutional framework.

Merrill Jensen, in The Articles of Confederation, noted the linkage between Jefferson's Declaration and the Articles of Confederation.

He wrote,

"The Articles were declared to be the constitutional expression of the philosophy of the Declaration, [Spirit of '76] which limited the central government to the sole power of determining war and peace, rule for capture, of settling disputes between two or more states concerning boundaries, jurisdictions, coining of money and regulating its value, managing affairs with Indians, of fixing the boundaries of new colonies, on the principles of liberty, appointing a Council of State of seven members." (1970.),

Jensen noted that the final draft of the Articles of Confederation, adopted 1777, contained the term "expressly delegated," a term that Madison intended to delete in his subsequent Bill of Rights, of 1791.

Article II. Each state retains its sovereignty, freedom and independence, and every Power, Jurisdiction and right, which is not by this confederation *expressly delegated to the United States*, in Congress assembled.

The final draft of the Articles also omitted congressional control of boundaries, charter claims and unallocated lands in the Northwest Territories.

The significance of this omission in the final draft of the Articles, in 1777, was the subsequent adoption, in 1787, by the Congress of the Confederacy, of the Northwest

Ordinance, that provided a path toward statehood for the territories, and more significantly prohibited slavery in the future states.

The Articles were defective from the unified coherent ruling class ideology, and the two major defects that Madison fixed in his new constitution concerned farmer insurrection and state-issued money.

The third major money defect, from the perspective of the natural aristocracy, concerned how to redeem the Revolutionary war bonds, at full face value.

That defect was fixed by Madison and Hamilton in 1791, with the creation of The Bank of the United States, a private, for-profit bank co-owned by the U. S. Government, and ruling class domestic and foreign investors.

And, it from this second perspective of the defects in the Articles, by the ruling class that the national narrative myth is promoted by the community of scholars who write about George Mason's opposition to Madison's rules, as if Mason's entire objection was simply that the document did not contain a Bill of Rights.

We agree with the thesis of Charles Beard that the Convention and the rules of the Constitution were the handiwork of a skillful group of elites, "whose property interests were immediately at stake." (Rutland, Robert Allen, The Ordeal of the Constitution: The Antifederalists and the Ratification Struggle of 1787-1788, University of Oklahoma Press, 1966.).

We extend Beard's thesis to add that the skillful group of elites had a coherent social class ideology which guided their work at the Convention, and continues to guide the American Ruling Class in financial plunder today.

We also add the point made by Rutland that the defects of the Articles, as seen from the perspective of the aristocracy, were made worse by the economic and financial behavior of the elites in undermining the functioning of the Articles, prior to Madison's calling for the Convention, after the Annapolis Convention of 1786.

According to outside foreign observers, the American natural aristocracy was subverting the government. That subversion of the rule of law culminated in the overthrow of the Articles, by members of the natural aristocracy, who attended the Convention.

Rutland notes,

"The French charge d affairs in New York placed much of the blame on the aristocratic clique which withheld support from the tottering Confederation."

Madison saw the American society as comprised of two social classes, creditors and debtors, who were in economic conflict with each other.

According to Michael Zuckert,

"Madison's conflict was expressed as the natural property rights of creditors versus the political rights of debtors, where the natural property rights are superior to the political rights that are derived from the higher status of property rights. Madison protected the minority rights of creditors against the majority rights of debtors." (Zuckert, Michael, The Natural Rights Republic: Studies In The Foundation of The American Political Tradition, University of Notre Dame Press, 1996.).

On June 19, 1787, early in the deliberations of the Convention, Alexander Hamilton expressed the social class conflict perspective that the ruling class used as the reasons for calling the Convention.

Hamilton stated,

"All communities divide themselves into the few and the many. The first are the rich and wellborn, the other the mass of the people…The people are turbulent and changing; they seldom judge or determine right. Give therefore to the first class a distinct, permanent share in the government. They will check the unsteadiness of the second, and as they cannot receive any advantage by a change, they therefore will ever maintain good government."

We argue that there is a much more accurate, simple and common sense reason for the natural aristocracy to call for the Convention.

Money.

Or, more specifically, Madison's intention to replace the Articles of Confederation with rules that made it easier for the natural aristocracy to use the agencies of government to make more money by creating rules for unlimited economic power of the government over common citizens.

There were three main money issues that Madison had to solve at the Convention.

First, he and Hamilton had to figure out how the worthless government bonds issued to finance the Revolution could be redeemed, by the natural aristocracy, at full face value.

Second, Madison had to stop state governments from printing their own worthless paper money, and make money issued by the U. S. Treasury the only legal tender in the nation.

Third, Madison had to prohibit farmers from engaging in rebellion when the farmers could not pay their debts and taxes in gold and silver, primarily because there was no gold and silver in circulation.

In other words, the three main defects that Madison and Hamilton fixed in the new constitutional rules concerned common citizen rebellion, repayment of government debt at full face value, and eliminating state issued money in favor of all legal tender issued by the central government, backed by the international market exchange value of gold and silver.

The major urgent precipitating factor for Madison in calling the Convention was the farmer's rebellion, late in 1786, in western Massachusetts, called Shays' Rebellion.

The historical context of Shays' Rebellion is the legislation in various states to provide debt relief to farmers who were not able to repay their loans in gold and silver.

Various state legislatures had been attempting to provide relief to farmers by passing laws which voided the contracts for loans made to farmers by banks and private investors.

In other words, prior to the Convention, a bank or private investor who had previously entered into a loan contract with a farmer, demanding repayment in gold and silver, could have the loan repayment obligation of the farmer rescinded or modified, by a subsequent law passed by the state legislature.

According to Michael Klarman, in his book. The Framers Coup, Madison thought that the farmer debt relief legislation was unfair to the ruling class.

Klarman wrote,

"Madison objected to the injustice of state legislation on creating paper money and debtor relief laws ... Madison viewed society as two classes: creditors or debtors, rich or poor… Madison declared that the Senate ought to come from and represent the wealth of the nation. The Senate should serve as a bastion of privilege." [to provide legal protection for the ruling class]. (Oxford University Press, 2016.).

When elites in the Massachusetts legislature ended the debt relief measures, in 1786, the farmers rebelled.

Rutland describes Shays' Rebellion,

"Shays' Rebellion was an armed uprising in Massachusetts (mostly in and around Springfield) during 1786 and 1787. Revolutionary War veteran Daniel Shays led four thousand rebels (called Shaysites) in an uprising against perceived economic and civil rights injustices. In 1787, the rebels marched on the United States' Armory at Springfield in an unsuccessful attempt to seize its weaponry and overthrow the government." (The Ordeal of the Constitution, 1966.).

Rutland cites Shays' Rebellion as a leading cause for Madison to convene the Convention, while Forrest McDonald, in his list of factors leading up to the Convention, cited above, omits, entirely, a reference to Shays' Rebellion.

According to David Stewart, in books The Summer of 1787: The Men Who Invented the Constitution, the farmers who could not find paper money or gold to pay their taxes and debts, were being thrown in jail and having their farm lands confiscated by the local courts.

Stewart writes,

"The rebels [common citizens] raged at a state government dominated by merchants who insisted on high taxes [paid in gold] to repay the state's war debts, then awarded seats in the State Senate on the basis of the wealth of each community...As many as 2/3 of them had been hauled into debtor's court, facing humiliation and even jail....their goal was the arsenal in Springfield...Angry farmers had closed courts in New Hampshire and Connecticut [to stop the courts from confiscating the farm land]. (Simon & Schuster, 2007.).

The rich men of Boston financed the counter insurgency against the farmers with their own funds, not tax revenue funds.

Stewart notes,

"The rich men of Boston passed the hat to undertake funding of a state force of 4,000 [soldiers] to march to western Massachusetts to quell the rebellion.

Stewart cites the farmer's rebellion as the main reason for Madison to convene the Convention.

Stewart writes,

"Shays and his neighbors provided a critical push in the effort to create a new American government." [to insure domestic tranquility].

Stewart cites General Washington's letter to Madison, in 1787, that the Rebellion was the reason for convening the Convention.

Stewart writes,

"What stronger evidence…[Washington to Madison] can be given of the want of energy in *our* ["royal' we] government than these disorders?"

The threat of common citizen rebellion was so strong that many elites, at the time, were contemplating the division of the Confederacy into three separate nations.

Stewart cites a 1786 letter by James Monroe,

"Certain it is that committees are held in this town [Boston] of Eastern men and others of New York, upon the subject of dismemberment of the states East of the Hudson from the Union and the erection of them into a separate government…Six months later Madison anticipated public support for a "partition of the Union into three more practicable and energetic governments."

Stewart notes that Mason was surprised by the anti-democratic passions of the delegates from Massachusetts, caused by Shays' Rebellion, when Mason arrived at the convention.

Stewart writes,

"Mason was surprised to find that the New Englanders, despite their reputations for democratic views, were almost anti-republican which he attributed to the "unexpected evils they experienced with Daniel Shays and his men…In the Convention's early days, the experience of Shays' Rebellion had made Gerry hostile to democracy. In Massachusetts, Gerry reported, "the worst men get into the legislature." They were, he continued, "men of indigence, ignorance and baseness, [who] spare no pains however dirty to carry their point against men who are superior to the artifices practiced."

The main cause that precipitated the farmer's rebellion was lack of currency and gold to pay their debts and taxes, which resulted in their lands being confiscated by judicial decree in local courts.

Stewart writes,

"In truth the lack of government revenue resulted in part from the crippling lack of currency...Without enough hard money in circulation, citizens like Shays rebels could not pay their taxes. forcing the state governments either to punish nonpayment of foregone revenue..[confiscate farms]...The government's impotence inflicted on every American twin plagues of bad money and confusing money. ..By July of 1779, a continental dollar was worth less 5 cents....Since Congress's money was worthless, the British pound was the prevailing currency...in Virginia the pound sterling held 1289 grams of silver, in Pennsylvania, only 1031....In 1785, Virginia pegged the US dollar at 6 shillings...New York and North Carolina set the value at 8 shillings...South Carolina and Georgia chose a value of 4 shillings and 6 pence."

The main reason that the 13 states did not have an adequate supply of money was that the American aristocracy had sent their wealth to England, for safe keeping.

One of the ways that the American natural aristocracy undermined the government, and caused the shortage of gold, prior to the Convention, was sending their silver specie and gold to England, primarily to the Bank of England.

The payment of debts, by farmers, in state-issued money was not acceptable to the natural aristocracy, because the paper money was not exchangeable in London, at the Bank of England.

Only gold and silver was acceptable as a medium of exchange in international trade between the American ruling class and the British ruling class.

And, the American ruling class had already sent their gold and silver to London, prior to Shays' Rebellion. Therefore, the ruling class wanted to be paid in gold and silver, not worthless paper money, issued by the states.

Rutland also cites Gerry's anti-democratic passion, after Shays' Rebellion, as the primary factor in convening the Convention.

Rutland writes,

"Daniel Shays' rebellious uprising in Massachusetts had been an unmistakable warning of the national temper. [of common citizens]. Elbridge Gerry of Massachusetts, the name of Daniel Shays still fresh in his memory, warned of the dangers of this "levilling spirit," but Mason gave no sign of disowning the Virginia Declaration of Rights. The Confederation allowed state legislatures to call the turn in national affairs; now he perceived, quite correctly, that changes being proposed would affect citizens more directly than ever before. That "all power is vested in, and consequently derived from, the people" moved him even to consider supporting popular elections for president, an advanced suggestion that he made no further show of favoring when it grew obvious that most of the Convention was appalled by it." (Rutland, 1966).

In his book, The Constitutional Convention of 1787: A Biographical Dictionary, Joseph C. Morton, cites the significance of Shay's Rebellion, in calling for the Convention, by writing,

"Shays Rebellion: [August 1786 – February 1787] This rebellion convinced many Americans [ruling class] of the need to establish a strong central government …that could squelch riotous behavior."

Helen Hill Miller noted that,

"Shays' Rebellion, had caused a reaction against democracy, particularly in New England, where earlier it had been most broadly practiced. As soon as the Convention turned to the proposition that the lower house of the national legislature be elected by the people of the states, Connecticut's Sherman declared his preference for choice by the state legislatures: "the people . . . should have as little to do as may be about the Government. They want [do not have] information and are constantly liable to be misled." Gerry of Massachusetts agreed: "The evils we experience flow from the excess of democracy. The people do not want [lack] virtue; but are the dupes of pretended patriots. [Mason]. He [Gerry] had been too republican. heretofore: he was still however republican, but had been taught by experience the danger of the levelling spirit." (Miller, Helen Hill, George Mason : Gentleman Revolutionary, UNC Press, 1975.).

At the time of the Convention, the natural aristocracy public relations campaign to cancel the reputation of George Mason had already begun, by deprecating Mason as a "Shayite."

Miller notes that,

"In October 1787, the Connecticut Courant reprinted a Philadelphia dispatch "that the Federalists should be distinguished hereafter by the name Washingtonians and the Antifederalists by the name Shayites, in every part of the United States."

Miller notes that the anti-democratic sentiments of Madison and Hamilton were well known, throughout the 13 states.

She cites Amos Singletary, who wrote in 1788,

"These lawyers and men of learning and monied men that talk so finely…expect to be the managers of this constitution, and get all the power and all the money into their hands, and then they will swallow up all us little folks, like the great Leviathan,"

Madison admitted to Jefferson, after the Convention ended, that his call for the Convention was linked to Shays' Rebellion.

Hill cites Madison,

"I am persuaded I do not err in saying that the evils issuing from these sources [Shays' Rebellion] contributed more to that uneasiness which produced the Convention, and prepared the public mind for a general reform, [coup] than those which accrued to our national character and interest from the Revolution…[The] inadequacy of the Confederation is its [Convention's] immediate object. A reform therefore which does not make provision for private rights, [Mason's proposed amendments] must be materially defective. The restraints agst. paper emissions, and violations of contracts are not sufficient. Supposing them to be effectual as far as they go, they are short of the mark. Injustice may be enacted by such an infinitude of legislative expedients, that where the imposition exists it can only be controuled by some provision which reaches all cases whatsoever."

Beginning in 1785, the U. S. economy entered into a three year economic collapse which devastated the financial interests of farmers.

The causes of the economic collapse lay in the speculative land investments by the ruling class, overexpansion of credit for farmers by banks and private investors, a postwar deflation in agricultural products, competition in the manufacturing sector from Britain, and lack of a sound monetary system.

The economic collapse of 1785, coupled with the lack of money in the economy, is the proximate cause of Shay's Rebellion.

The farmers in Massachusetts did not have any money to repay their debts to the Ruling Class, and as a result of not being repaid their loans to farmers, the natural aristocracy met in Philadelphia and agreed to replace the Articles of Confederation.

The social and economic conditions of low economic growth in January of 1787 led to greater levels of social class conflict between elites, who desired to maintain their incomes, and the working social classes, described by William Sumner as the 'forgotten man.''.

The new constitutional rules eviscerated the authority of state governments to issue currency and imposed centralized national rules over the law of contracts.

The political institutional structure, created by Madison, granted unelected political power to Hamilton's Bank of the United States, modeled on the Bank of England, and members of the American natural aristocracy, who used the agencies of government to maintain their incomes through crony capitalist control over money supply, government taxes and government spending.

The two factors for Madison calling the Convention are related.

The threat of civil unrest by farmers, coupled with the issuance of paper currency by state legislatures, were the two predominant factors that prompted Madison to call the Convention.

Madison inserted the text "insure domestic tranquility" into the Preamble after September 15, 1787, but before the morning of September 17, 1787, to provide the Federal Government with the police power to quell any such further dissent by common citizens.

The first time Mason saw the new text of the Preamble was the morning of September 17.

Madison and Hamilton empowered the military to attack citizens who were considered by the natural aristocracy to be "insurrectionists," which they did in 1794, when an army of 13,000 soldiers marched to Western Pennsylvania, under the command of Alexander Hamilton, to quell the farmer's Whiskey Rebellion, because the farmers were refusing to pay their debts in gold and silver.

We argue that the monetary system in the Confederacy, prior to the Convention, was not beyond repair, under the authority of the Articles of Confederation.

For example, the monetary system could have been fixed with a unified state-banking system that cooperated on the definition of legal tender, across state boundaries.

Already, prior to the Convention, states were cooperating on trade, navigation and fishing regulations and agreements.

In 1785, Mason and George Washington hosted the Mount Vernon Conference to work with the state of Maryland on a comprehensive 13-point plan on the use of the Potomac River and Chesapeake Bay.

In 1781, the Congress chartered the nation's first national bank, which had many of the same features as Hamilton's 1791 Bank of the United States.

As Jack Rakove notes,

"In fact, the Continental Congress did establish the Bank of North America in Philadelphia in 1781. Yet because Congress lacked the authority to tax, it could not make enough deposits in the bank to adequately support it. Other banks were founded in Boston, New York, and Baltimore later in the decade, but few Americans really understood how banks actually worked. Many skeptics worried about the financial power banks could wield." (Rakove, Jack, Original Meanings: Politics and Ideas in the Making of the Constitution A.A. Knopf, 1996.).

The alternative to overthrowing the Articles of Confederation would have been continuing with the operation of the Bank of North America, with state cooperation on taxation, which the states had demonstrated their ability to cooperate in the passage of the Northwest Territories Act.

In 1787, prior to the Convention, all 13 states cooperated on the definition of new states entering the Confederacy in the Northwest Territories.

We argue that the 13 states would have cooperated with each other on the issue of taxation, if they had realized that it was Madison's intent to overthrow the Articles.

Farmers were also solving, on their own initiative, issues related to the lack of currency to conduct their farming trade.

Josephine Pacheco describes how common citizens were engaged in barter and forms of substitute currency to conduct their business.

Pacheco writes,

"Very early in the development of the Virginia and Maryland colonies, bills of exchange based on tobacco became accepted currency. Rice and indigo served the same purpose in South Carolina, as did rum and molasses in the northern colonies. John McCusker describes colonial trade as basically "multilateral arrangements designed indirectly to establish credits in London on which to draw bills [payments for commodities]… For over 150 years, the colonists tried "to repair the defects in their money supply" by barter, by assessing monetary value to commodities, by overvaluing what little coin they had, and by issuing paper money." (Pacheco, Josephine, Antifederalism: The Legacy of George Mason, ed., George Mason University Press, 1992.).

During the Convention, Mason was in favor of a unified monetary system, as long as the creation and control of the currency system remained under the control of the elected House of Representatives, and not under the control of the appointed Senate.

Donald Senese, in George Mason and the Legacy of Constitutional Liberty, writes,

"Nothing was as important [to Mason] as limiting money policy to the House of Representatives. He returned to that over and over, during the entire summer. Mason understood, better than any other member of the Convention, that where the money was, there also was the power. Since the House of Representatives was the only body directly responsive to the will of the people, [Mason argued] that it alone should have the authority to determine how the people's money would be spent." (George Mason and the Legacy of Constitutional Liberty: An Examination of the Influence of George Mason on the American Bill of Rights, Editor, Fairfax County History Commission, 1989.).

George Mason made his arguments against the Constitution in the context of the interest and principle repayments of the Revolutionary War debt.

"Will it not be the duty of the Federal Court to say," said Mason, "that such state laws [granting farmer debt relief] are prohibited? This goes to the destruction and annihilation of all the citizens of the United States, to enrich a few."

The worthless government bonds had been issued to common citizens as payment for fighting in the Revolutionary War. The bonds were designed to pay both principle and interest to the owner over an extended period of time.

The bonds were tradable instruments that could be used as currency by the soldiers to pay for farm expenses.

So, in addition to barter and the use of farm commodities as a substitute for money, the farmers used their bonds as currency, in exchange for goods and services.

The full face value of the bonds, on the day they were issued to the soldiers, was $100.

The soldiers sold their bonds to wealthy citizens for as little as $20 a bond.

The concentration of ownership in the hands of the ruling class was extreme.

According to Helen Hill Miller

"Both national and state securities had been largely bought. up by men of capital [ruling class] at vastly depreciated prices; and while assumption [new federal government taking over payment of principle and interest on the bonds] might be good news in some states, it was not so in Virginia. Madison confirmed to. Pendleton that the commonwealth [Virginia] although it had already made progress in retiring its own obligations from its own resources, Virginia would become liable for a prorated share of the outstanding debt of states that had accomplished far less." [progress in paying off the bonds principle and interest] (George Mason: Gentleman Revolutionary, UNC Press, 1975).

In Maryland, fewer than 50 wealthy citizens had bought up 50% all bonds issued to soldiers, by the beginning of the Convention.

Madison and Hamilton intended to use the proposed Bank of the United States as the vehicle to redeem all bonds at full face value of $100.

Rutland notes that Mason was adamantly opposed to this scheme to use the proposed Bank to buy back the bonds from the wealthy citizens at full face value.

Rutland writes,

"He [Mason] thought the Constitution as worded would carry the implicit promise to redeem depreciated government obligations at par and would beget speculations and increase the pestilent practice of stockjobbing." [real bills doctrine]. (George Mason: Reluctant Statesman, LSU Press, 1961.).

Mason correctly predicted that the new government would create a will of its own, independent of the will of the citizens.

He stated at the Convention, during the debate on government bonds,

"These gentlemen [Federalists] who will be elected senators, will fix themselves in the federalist town, and become citizens of that town more than of your state."

From as early as 1779, Hamilton had been writing documents that federal assumption of state revolution war debt, at full face value, would be a "national blessing."

During the Convention, Madison and Hamilton wrote the passages of the new constitution to accomplish this end, with the added asset of the creation of Hamilton's Bank of the United States to print money and handle the bond transactions on behalf of the new government.

According to Saul Cornell, in The Other Founders,

"Hamilton's plan called for redeeming the full face value of depreciated federal securities, which would have generated enormous profit for speculators…The government would deposit its funds in the bank and supervise its operations, the directors would be drawn from private stockholders. The bank would print money and back a national currency." (UNC Press, 1999.).

The wealthy delegates to the Convention were well aware of the investment "get-rich-quick" scheme of buying the bonds low, at pennies on the dollar and selling them high, at a guaranteed profit.

David Stewart wrote that delegates to the Convention were advising their states to engage in this risk free, guaranteed-profitable investment.

"A New Hampshire delegate expected the Constitution would bolster the value of public debt and paper currency. In an eighteenth-century version of insider trading (though for the benefit of public entities), he urged his state's governor to get a jump on the market by having towns buy back their devalued bonds and notes: otherwise, the state would be obliged to buy [them from] brokers, hawkers, speculators and stock jockeys at six or perhaps eight times their present value." (The Summer of 1787: The Men Who Invented the Constitution, 2007.).

At the end of the Convention, Mason wrote to James Monroe that,

"Our new Government is a government of Stock-jobbing. and Favouritism. It required no extraordinary Degree of Penetration, to foresee that it would be so."

After the Virginia ratification convention, in 1788, Mason told Jefferson that Hamilton had "done us more injury than Great Britain and all her fleets and armies."

As early as 1780, Hamilton was targeting farmers for an increased tax burden.

Hamilton saw the "farmers" as a collectivist social class, just as he imagined the natural aristocracy saw themselves as a social class, with a coherent class ideology.

In 1780, New York Congress delegate James Duane asked Hamilton to analyze "the defects of our present [financial] system." Hamilton replied with a lengthy letter assessing the various errors Congress had made and proposing the remedies he thought necessary.

Excerpts From Alexander Hamilton's letter to James Duane:

"The quantity of money formerly in circulation among us is estimated at about thirty millions of dollars. This was barely sufficient for our interior commerce. Our exterior commerce was chiefly carried on by barter. We sent our commodities abroad and brought back others in return. The ballance of the principal branch was against us; and the little specie derived from others was transferred directly to the payment of that ballance without passing into home circulation…Including loan-office certificates and state emissions, we have about 400.000.000 of dollars in circulation. The real value of these is less than 7.000.000, which is the true circulating medium of these states;…

… The Farmers have the game in their own hands and will make it very difficult to lower the prices of their commodities. For want of labourers there is no great superfluity of the most essential articles raised. These are things of absolute necessity and must be purchased as well by the other classes [ruling class] of the society as by the public. The farmers on the contrary, if they do not like the price are not obliged to sell because they have almost every necessary within themselves, salt and one or two more excepted, which bear a small proportion to what is wanted from them and which they can obtain by barter for other articles equally indispensible. **Heavy taxes**, it may be said will oblige them to sell but they can pay with a small part of what they have any taxes our legislatures will venture to impose or would be able to inforce…

… One measure alone can counter-ballance these advantages of the Farmers and oblige them to ***contribute their proper quota*** to the support of government; a tax in kind. This ought instantly to begin throughout the states. The present quantity of cash though nominally enormous would in reality be found incompetent to domestic circulation were it not that a great part of our internal commerce is carried on by barter. For this reason it is impossible by pecuniary taxes to raise a sum proportioned to the wants of the state. The money is no longer a general representative, and when it ceases to be so, ***the state ought to call for a portion of the thing represented; or in other words to tax in kind***. This will greatly facilitate whatever plan of finance is adopted, because it will lessen the expenditures in cash and make it the easier to retain what is drawn in." [emphasis in excerpt added]

Hamilton was proposing the confiscation of the farmer's crops, in lieu of taxes paid in cash, because the farmers did not have any money. In addition to the earlier tax collection technique of confiscating the farmer's land for non-tax payment, Hamilton's plan was to confiscate the in-kind value of their crops so that they would "contribute their proper quota."

Klarman notes that, in 1794, after Hamilton had successfully implemented his plan, the U. S. Government cracked down on farmers in Western Pennsylvania for not paying their fair share of taxes in gold and silver.

"When government cracked down on enforcement of paying taxes in specie, tens of thousands of farmers lost their farms…70% of farmers on some Pennsylvania counties saw their property foreclosed upon…As much as 10% of the population in one Pennsylvania region were in debtors prison." (The Framers Coup, 2016.).

In addition to Hamilton's predatory view of the social class interests of farmers, Hamilton also explains that the intended beneficiaries of his scheme are wealthy citizens.

Hamilton concludes his letter:

"The only plan that can preserve the currency is one that will make it the immediate interest of the monied men [natural aristocracy] to cooperate with government in its support."

Hamilton's economic theory anticipates Marxian labor theory of value, in Das Kapital [1867] by about 90 years.

Hamilton notes that,

"…The relative value of m⟨oney⟩ being determined by the greater or less ⟨portion⟩ of labor and commodities which it ⟨will pur⟩chase, whatever these gained in price⟨, that of⟩ course lost in value."

Hamilton also anticipates the totalitarian government of communism in his idea that the farmers are serfs whose work product is owned by the state, and whose crops can be confiscated the state.

Hamilton's model for the American political system was British social class system, and his model of the American financial system was the Bank of England.

Rakove notes that Hamilton, in his letter to Duane, explains how the Bank of England works to enrich the British nobility through funding military imperialism.

Rakove notes that Hamilton wrote in his letter,

"The inspiration for this idea came from Great Britain. One critical element in the development of British imperial power in the eighteenth century had been the creation of a national bank in 1694. "The Bank of England unites public authority and faith with private credit," Hamilton wrote, "and hence we see what a vast fabric of paper credit is raised on a visionary basis." Why could Americans not try the same "experiment?" (Original Meanings: Politics and Ideas in the Making of the Constitution, 1996.).

Rakove adds,

"The success of the eighteenth-century British Empire was the model that knowledgeable observers wanted to apply, and Hamilton understood its lessons well."

Madison fixed the three money issues in the Articles of Confederation.

First, he inserted both the phrase "insure domestic tranquility," and the "necessary and proper clause," to extend the scope of constitutional jurisdiction, so that there would be no effective limit on the authority of the government to quell dissent or print money.

Later, in 1991, Madison deleted the term "expressly delegated," from Article 10 of the Bill of Rights.

In Article I. Section 8, Madison wrote that the new government had the monopoly power to coin money, and to borrow an unlimited amount of money, in the form of bonds.

The monopoly to coin money was combined with Hamilton's monopoly at the Bank of the United States as the exclusive agent for managing the government's bonds, and for printing money.

Hamilton's legal charter from Congress to form the First Bank included a provision that only the notes on loans issued by the Bank were accepted as legal tender when paying federal taxes, which the First Bank was in charge of collecting.

Article I, Section 8. To borrow Money on the credit of the United States; To regulate Commerce with foreign Nations, and among the several States… To coin money, regulate the Value thereof, and of foreign Coin, and fix the standard of Weights and Measures…

In Article I, Section 10, Madison prohibited the payment of taxes in paper money, and mandated the payment of taxes in gold and silver.

Article I, Section 10, Clause 1:

No State shall enter into any Treaty, Alliance, or Confederation; grant Letters of Marque and Reprisal; coin Money; emit Bills of Credit; make any Thing but gold and silver Coin a Tender in Payment of Debts; pass any Bill of Attainder, ex post facto Law, or Law impairing the Obligation of Contracts, or grant any Title of Nobility.

Madison also slipped into the text of Section 10, at the last moment, the "Impairment of Contracts" clause, which performed double duty for the natural aristocracy.

First, the contract clause prohibited state governments from offering debt relief to farmers in legislation that modified loan contracts.

Second, in conjunction with Madison's secret insertion of the Fugitive Slave Clause, the Impairment of Contracts clause made all slave-owner contracts to buy and sell slaves the law of the land, even in states which had banned slavery.

Madison's fixes worked in conjunction with the creation of Hamilton's bank, to provide the new government with unlimited power.

The three major empowering clauses for Madison's text were:

- Insure domestic tranquility.
- Necessary and proper clause.
- General welfare clause.
- War powers clause.

According to Rakove,

"In Hamilton's view, the Constitution vested the national government with "implied, as well as express powers." Without that reading of the text, the very ends for which the Constitution had been written would often prove unattainable."

The very ends for which the Constitution had been written, was to empower the financial power of the natural aristocracy permanently over the financial interests of common citizens.

Rakove notes,

"In his "Report on Manufactures" of December 5, 1791, for example, Hamilton wrote that "the power [granted to Congress] to raise money is plenary, and indefinite; and the objects to which it may be appropriated are no less comprehensive." This, he argued, was the real meaning of the general welfare clause. The phrase "General Welfare … necessarily embraces a vast variety of particulars, which are susceptible neither of specification nor of definition."…Likewise, the Commerce Clause, which was intended to regulate commerce between states to promote free trade, became inclusive of all commerce under Hamilton's interpretation. And as taxes need tax collectors, and none are more effective than armed ones, he took the "war powers" clause and extended it to mean a standing army in peacetime. Under the constitutional power to "provide for the common Defence," Congress has no restraints in providing resources to the military, or as he put it in Federalist No. 23, "These powers ought to exist without limitation, because it is impossible to foresee or define the extent and variety of national exigencies, or the correspondent extent and variety of the means which may be necessary to satisfy them."

Hamilton saw common citizens as a social class to be controlled by the agents of government.

Rakove noted that the Whiskey Act, of 1791, was as much an initiative to obtain tax revenues to pay the national debt at full face value, as it was to discipline the farmers.

Rakove writes,

Hamilton "justified" the Whiskey Act of March 3, 1791, as a means of servicing the national debt, [full face value] but then qualified his statement by saying the tax would be more useful as "a measure of social discipline than as a source of revenue." When citizens compared the hated tax to the British Stamp Act of 1765 and began tarring and feathering tax collectors, he [Hamilton] personally accompanied [as the commanding general of the military force] a 13,000-man federal army of conscripts to western Pennsylvania to show the rebellious small distillers, who bore a disproportionate share of the tax, what he meant by "social discipline."

Rakove notes that,

"Secretary of State Thomas Jefferson, renewed the arguments against the chartering of a national bank. In his view, the word "necessary" in the necessary and proper clause meant something more than convenient or very useful. Its true meaning in this case, Jefferson thought, was closer to indispensable. If Congress had other ways to secure its objectives, a nationally incorporated bank was unnecessary and improper. He also thought that a national bank was unconstitutional because the Tenth Amendment reserved all unenumerated powers to the states." (Jefferson,

Thomas Opinion on the Constitutionality of the Bill for Establishing a National Bank, 1791.)

"I consider the foundation of the Constitution as laid on this ground that "all powers not delegated to the U.S. by the Constitution, not prohibited by it to the states, are reserved to the states or to the people" [Tenth Amendment]. To take a single step beyond the boundaries thus specially drawn around the powers of Congress, is to take possession of a boundless field of power, no longer susceptible of any definition."

Jefferson was incorrect in his opinion that the 10th Amendment reserved "all unenumerated powers to the states."

Among the other issues Madison fixed with his new constitution, he also fixed the Tenth Amendment by deleting the text "expressly delegated," which had been Article II in the Articles of Confederation.

Chief Justice Marshall subsequently agreed with Madison's text in the 10th Amendment by ruling that, in the absence of the text "expressly delegated," the Government had unlimited "implied" powers to do whatever it wanted, untethered from any notion of "consent of the governed."

To review how Madison's rules and Hamilton's economic system worked in tandem to benefit the wealthy families, first Madison eliminated the ability of state banks to issue currency.

Second, Madison adopted a contract clause that made evasion of paying debts in gold or silver illegal. Debts and taxes had to be paid in gold and silver.

Third, Hamilton restricted the issuance of gold and silver coins, and established that only notes issued by his bank were deemed legal tender for paying taxes.

The farmers were left without either gold or paper currency to pay their debts.

Madison's text must be interpreted, and seen from the natural aristocracy perspective of creating a monetary and banking system that benefitted the natural aristocracy.

The part of Madison's Preamble about "promote the general Welfare, and secure the Blessings of Liberty to *ourselves and our* Posterity, refers to their own social class liberty, not common citizen liberty.

However, the national narrative myth of historians is used to obscure Mason's philosophy that liberty meant equal rights for all.

In order to have liberty for all citizens, Madison would have been required to reference "equal liberty," somewhere in the text, and referenced the prior authority of Jefferson's Declaration.

Madison's rules on representation made certain that, in the extended republic, common citizens would never develop a social class awareness, while his rules strengthened the social class consciousness of the Ruling Class in the concentrated power of the Senate and the unchecked power of the President.

The major compromise at the Convention of 1787 was not big states versus little states, or adding a bill of rights.

The major compromise was reconciling the ruling class interests of the Southern plantation aristocracy with the Northern commercial ruling class interests in banking and international trade.

Preserving slavery in the South, for the slaveocracy, was essential to protecting banking and commercial elite interests in the North

John Taylor of Caroline wrote in 1795, that Hamilton's system of debt funding was intended to,

"Accumulate wealth in a few hands. [The Bank] was a political moneyed engine used as a suppression of the republican state assemblies by manipulation of paper [money] interest."

Writing in Sketch of the Finances of the US, Albert Gallatin, wrote,

"The Bank had become a political engine and instead of adding to the capital of the US it had actually drained capital away from productive investment." (Gallatin, Albert, A Sketch of the Finances of the United States, W.A. Davis, 1796.).

Gallatin differentiated between productive private capital investments and financial manipulation, attacking speculators who lived to consume, to spend more than available."

Gallatin was offering an early critique of Hamilton's banking doctrine of "real bills."

Essentially, the real bills doctrine guided ruling class bankers for about 200 years. It is a rule purporting to link the future money supply to the future value of production, via short term commercial business loans called "bills of exchange," or simply bank loans collateralized by the expected future returns of the investments.(Vass, Laurie

Thomas, America's Final Revolution: Reconstructing Jefferson's American Dream of An Entrepreneurial Capitalist Society, Gabby Press, 2022.).

According to the doctrine, if bankers always based their judgment for a loan on "real bills" of future economic productivity, real productive output in the future would generate a real supply of future money, that would automatically equate the future supply of money with the future demand for money.

Real bills would end up without causing inflation in commodity or retail prices, in the current time period, because, in some prior period of time, the very smart bankers had limited their loans to real productive investments.

The doctrine states that money supply can never be excessive when issued against short-term commercial bills arising from real investments in goods.

In other words, inflationary over-issue of money is impossible provided credit is issued on loans made to finance real, productive investments, not wildly speculative investments, for example in building railroads or speculation on real estate on Indian territory.

In his review of the creation of Hamilton's economy, Richard Bernstein posed the basic political question raised by the rules created by Madison and Hamilton:

"Was it dangerous in a democratic government, to have important officers insulated from control by the people, or was it necessary to accept that risk [of aristocratic tyranny] in order to protect fundamental rights from infringement by popular passions or political intrigue?" (The Founding Fathers Reconsidered, Oxford University Press, 2011.)

The real bills doctrine of Hamilton is a false economic theory and leads the U.S. economy to collapse about every 10 years, because real bills does not yield real economic growth, it produces an over-supply of money, speculation in risky assets, inflation and economic collapse.

The Constitution of 1787 could have been written with economic rules that produced real economic growth, based upon private capital investment in private enterprise.

James Buchanan, in the next chapter offers insight into how another set of constitutional rules would lead to real economic growth that benefits all social classes, not rules which benefit the natural aristocracy.

Buchanan's new constitutional rules would begin where the Articles of Confederation ended, by states *expressly delegating* only certain powers and authority to the central government, in a state-sovereignty constitution, governed by Mason's principle that all legitimate authority is derived from the consent of the governed.

Chapter 5. James Buchanan's Individual Rights Constitutional Rules For Maximum Social Prosperity.

Our main economic argument in favor of using Mason's version of the American constitution is that it would have led to the emergence of a stable middle class social order, which would have eliminated the ruling class' justification to seek unearned advantage [shared plunder] through unelected power to manipulate money supply and interest rates.

The central bank's unelected power to manipulate the money supply and interest rates benefits the elite social classes, but leads to chronic economic instability in the American economy, with a recurring boom-bust cycle about every 10 years. (Vass, Laurie Thomas, America's Final Revolution: Reconstructing Jefferson's American Dream of An Entrepreneurial Capitalist Society, Gabby Press, 2022.).

Mason objected to Madison's consolidated all powerful central government, and insisted that Madison's constitution violated the spirit of liberty of the American Revolution.

We rely on the constitutional economic theory of James Buchanan to build out the details of what Mason's philosophy of individual freedom, would look like in a new decentralized state sovereignty constitutional framework.

The main point of Buchanan's public choice theory is that voluntary obedience to the "rule" of law leads to a stable social order where each individual, pursuing their own interests, leads to a distribution of wealth and income that is considered fair because citizens agreed to the creation of the constitutional rules that benefit all citizens.

The resulting emergence of a stable order occurs, after the constitution is created, when citizens engage in free market exchange to improve their own welfare.

We begin by imagining that American citizens are in a hypothetical state of nature, in 1776, when the Patriots first began discussing what form of government would replace the British monarchy.

We place their discussions about the form of government into Buchanan's two-step process of first defining the constitutional rules of the economic and political game, and then allow market and political exchange to create the ensuing market and political institutions.

We ask: If citizens in America, in 1776, had been provided the opportunity to follow Buchanan's rules for creating a new constitution, relying on Mason's individualist ideology, what would the market and social institutional structure of the new government look like.

We conclude that Buchanan's concept of creating constitutional rules would lead to an institutional stable social order, based upon voluntary citizen cooperation, which would not require the police state oppression of Leviathan to compel obedience to the rule of law.

We argue that there is only one configuration of constitutional rules, and only one method of citizen participation in the making of fair constitutional rules, that creates maximum rates of economic growth, and maximum diffusion of income benefits to all social classes of citizens.

That single constitutional configuration creates the maximum level of trust among citizens, so that citizens can trust each other to obey the rule of law.

It also creates the maximum rates of knowledge creation and diffusion among citizens.

Maximum rates of knowledge creation create maximum rates of technology innovation, which we argue in the next chapter on Schumpeter's entrepreneurial capitalist economy, leads to the greatest rates of economic growth.

Technological innovation, as suggested by Solow, accounted for most of the economic growth in the first part of the 20th Century, in the American economy.

We add the proviso to Schumpeter's evolutionary entrepreneurial theory that the most important technological innovation occurs within 50 miles of major metropolitan regions.

We argue that Mason's concept of individual liberty would be a better pathway to form a new constitution, today, after Madison's representative republic collapsed in the corrupt election of 2020.

A new constitution, with Mason's concept of individual liberty, placed within Buchanan's constitutional framework, and Schumpeter's entrepreneurial capitalist economy provides a pathway for American citizens out of the Marxist Democrat Leviathan.

Madison's constitution was based upon the British social class conflict model.

Buchanan's constitution is based upon social cooperation, not conflict, among individuals who are seeking to improve their own financial condition through free market exchange with other individuals.

Both types of constitutions are based upon a concept of social contract theory, beginning with Thomas Hobbes' Leviathan, in 1651.

Hobbes was trying to figure out what form of social order would replace either monarchy, or the institutional Christian Church.

In the absence of the social order provided by monarchy or the Church, Hobbes argued that society would be a lawless war of all against all, and that everyone therefore benefits by agreeing to obey a government committed to preventing such strife.

Hobbes, like Madison, argued that society was made up of social classes, not individual citizens,

Hobbes, like Madison, argued that society can be made orderly and productive only by a powerful central government in possession of a great deal of discretionary authority to issue commands about citizen obedience to the rule of law.

In Madison's version of social order, the powerful central government must be the exclusive dominion of the natural aristocracy.

In Buchanan's constitutional economics, in contrast, to Madison's collectivism, individual citizens examine the choice of pre-constitutional rules.

Buchanan calls decisions on what those rules should be "pre-constitutional decisions," because those rules are the rules of the game for all citizens, under the equal application of the law.

After the pre-constitutional decisions are made, individual citizens are free to make choices within the set of rules, which are called "post-constitutional decisions."

The post-constitutional rules define the market and political institutions that aim at three goals:

1. rewarding good work.
2. allowing for just deserts.
3. providing incentives to work.

As noted by Brennan and Buchanan,

"Individuals are recognized to possess their own privately determined objectives, their own life plans, and these need not be common to all persons. In this setting, [institutional] rules have the function of facilitating interactions among persons who may desire quite different things." (Brennan,

Geoffrey and Buchanan, James M., The Reason of Rules: Constitutional Political Economy, Cambridge University Press, 2008.).

The very nature of fair constitutional rules is that they guide individual choice to improve individual welfare, under conditions of future economic and market uncertainty.

We rely on the definition of constitutional order provided by Knut Wicksell that the ultimate goals of the new constitution are equality before the law, the greatest possible individual liberty, and peaceful cooperation of all people in the pursuit of their life's sovereign mission.

The fundamental difference between Madison's version of the constitution and Mason's version is the distinction between individualism and group collectivism.

In Mason's constitution, the emphasis is on cooperation between individuals, rather than Madison's social class conflict interaction between common citizens and the ruling class.

Buchanan postulates three conditions on the creation of an individualist constitution.

First, Buchanan stipulates that individuals in the society are rational in the pursuit of their life's mission.

Rationality means that the decisions made by individuals in the market or in politics, promote the welfare of the individual, and that the decisions are not irrational, in the sense that individuals make decisions that undermine or subvert their sovereign life mission.

Second, Buchanan stipulates that only human individuals make choices, and that the choices of individuals can be aggregated together to determine what all individual citizens value in the market or in the political system.

Buchanan relies on the tradition of Adam Smith that the decisions of individuals, all pursuing their own individual interests and possessing only their own unique bits of knowledge, come to have their plans and actions coordinated, chiefly by adjustments in market prices and the resulting profits and losses made in business decisions.

Buchanan, like Mason, believed that each individual is morally equal to every other individual. Because no person is superior, ethically or morally, to any other person, no person's opinions or preferences should be given special advantage over those of other persons.

Madison, like Hobbes, assumed that the interest of the state, or central government, is identical to that of society. Thus, in Madison's constitution, any policy made by the ruling class that strengthened the state was believed to also strengthen society.

For Buchanan, society improves normatively the more reliably it gives to each individual, regardless of intelligence, wealth, rank, or any other social class distinction, an equal say in the affairs of government, with the scope and powers of government expressly delegated to the government, by the consent of the governed, in the creation of the pre-constitutional rules.

Third, Buchanan stated that there was no imaginary social welfare function that existed independently of the decisions made by individuals in the market or political system.

Buchanan stated that there is no hypothetical macro-economic concept, such as Rousseau's general will or a Bergsonian social welfare function, beyond the welfare of each of the individuals in the society that created the pre-constitutional rules.

In Madison's version of constitutional rules, a set of ruling class elites judge the fairness of welfare outcomes, after economic exchange has occurred, as if there is an independent social welfare function that they intend to maximize by moving income from one social class to another.

In Madison's rules, the ruling class elites shift income and economic resources to different social class groups, based upon the changing shape of their imaginary social welfare function.

Paul Aligica, in Exploring The Political Economy and Social Philosophy of James M. Buchanan, notes that,

"Buchanan and Tullock's critique [of Madison's constitutional rules] emphasizes that,

(1) no objective social welfare function exists;
(2) that even if one existed, "societies" do not choose how to maximize social welfare; only individuals make choices; and
(3) that individuals within the political sector, and in the private market, act purposefully, basing their choices on their private assessment of costs and benefits of their decisions to maximize individual welfare. (Rowman & Littlefield, 2018.).

Buchanan rejected Madison's assumption that the state is a benevolent overlord of the individuals who comprise the governed.

The agencies of the state, or the ruling class officials chosen to execute the administration of government, are not driven by virtuous values that would lead to decisions that benefit common citizens.

Rather, Buchanan states that the welfare and financial interests of elected representatives and agents of the state maximize is their own personal welfare, in Madison's shared plunder spoils system of rewards.

Since there is no grand social welfare function that guides the behavior of elites, in Madison's constitution, they substitute their own social class consciousness, as if that behavior is a surrogate for a social welfare function, based upon the logic that whatever improves the welfare of the elites also improves the welfare of the state.

There is no force or constraint [checks and balances] in Madison's constitution that acted to restrain government from expanding its power to obtain financial benefits for the natural aristocracy.

Buchanan's constitution aims at the creation of rules, in the pre-constitutional setting, that limits the power of government to exclusively providing the functions of property-rights protection and public-goods provision, without overstepping its limits into civil rights predation or wealth redistribution.

In The Reason of Rules, Brennan and Buchanan criticize Madison's rules precisely because it contained unlimited implied powers to obtain the ends of government, which in reality meant obtaining the welfare benefits of the ruling class.

They write,

"Our specific claim is that justice takes its meaning from the rules for the social order within which notions of justice are to be applied. To appeal to considerations of [constitutional] justice is to appeal to relevant [constitutional] rules… To the extent that this (Madison's existing) constitution commands little respect, in part because it is seen to fail in its function of limiting the scope of both governmental and private intrusion into what are widely held to be protected spheres of activity."
(The Reason of Rules: Constitutional Political Economy, 2008.).

Brennan and Buchanan's remedy for Madison's open-ended special interest tyranny relies on the potential for changes in the pre-constitutional market and political rules that constrains the power of the central government.

"These [pre-constitutional] rules provide the framework within which [the post-constitutional institutional] patterns of distributional end states emerge from the interaction of persons who play various complex functional [market and political] roles."

In other words, Buchanan's constitution would severely limit the central government's range of power so that citizen free choice in subsequent market and political institutions would allow a stable social order to emerge.

In leaving the imaginary state of nature to form a constitution, Buchanan imagines the logical method that citizens would use to agree on pre-constitutional rules.

In Constitutional Economics, Buchanan described this feature of citizen agreement of fair and just pre-constitutional rules.

Accepting the first premise that individuals are rational in the pursuit of their own sovereign life mission, Buchanan relies on a philosophy of logic to explain how the end goals, clearly stated in a constitution create the binding allegiance of all citizens to follow the rule of law.

Buchanan writes,

"Uncertainty about just where one's own interest will lie in a sequence of plays or rounds will lead a rational person, from his own interest, to prefer rules and arrangements, or constitutions that will seem fair, no matter what final positions he might occupy." (Buchanan, James M., Constitutional Economics, Blackwell Publishing, 1991.).

In leaving the state of nature, and forming a constitution, individuals are placed in a position of uncertainty in the outcome of their life's mission.

No individual knows in advance where the individual may end up, given the choice between one set of constitutional rules or another.

In other words, fair and just rules, in the pre-constitutional setting are derived because any individual citizen is uncertain about where she may end up in the future market.

Buchanan relies upon the rationality of self-interest as a force that binds individuals to society as a process of rationally minimizing risk in uncertain future decision making environments. (Buchanan, James, The Logical Foundations of Constitutional Liberty, Liberty Fund, 1999.).

A rational individual, with a rational self-interest, would choose fair rules for all, aimed at the greatest freedom for all.

In constitutional decision-making under uncertainty, individuals would seek to implement fair rules that had maximum equal rights for all, with special privileges for none.

The end goal, or teleos, of the constitutional rules, in this case of rational self-interest, is individual freedom, which leads to maximum social prosperity.

Buchanan's premise of citizen rationality applies to both the future economic market, as well as the future political market of voting.

Each voter would choose political rules in the pre-constitutional setting, from behind the veil of uncertainty, ignorant of their future positions in the society that the voter may occupy.

In making pre-constitutional political rules, citizens would choose fair rules of democratic citizen participation in order for the ensuing political and market institutions to coordinate mutually beneficial social outcomes for all citizens.

In terms of justice and fairness of constitutional rules, Paul Aligica writes,

"[Buchanan's] Constitutional political economy teaches us that the rules of the game (pre-constitutional-choices) are more important for reaching socially desirable outcomes than are the strategies that players may use within a given set of rules. [post-constitutional]. Therefore, sustainable reforms come from changes to the [pre-constitutionl] rules of governance as opposed to policy changes within the existing rules of governance."(Exploring The Political Economy and Social Philosophy of James M. Buchanan, 2018.).

The practical implication of Aligica's insight is that Madison's unfair rules, which never obtained legitimate citizen consent, must be replaced by fair constitutional rules, in which citizens have an equal opportunity to participate in the creation, and the approval, of the new constitution.

Roger Congleton explains the logical connection between citizen equality before the law and the fairness and legitimacy of pre-constitutional rules.

Congleton writes,

"Collective action at the constitutional level of analysis produces both property right systems (civil law) and collective decision-making systems (political institutions). The legitimacy of [consent of pre-constitutional] collective action in general and constitutional governance in particular requires individuals to be fundamentally equal in their roles as citizens at the constitutional level of choice and also in the civil [and market] society framed by the constitutions chosen." (Congleton, Roger D., The Contractarian Constitutional Political Economy of James Buchanan, West Virginia University Press, 2013.).

Buchanan predicts that fair pre-constitutional rules will allow for the emergence of a stable political and economic society through voluntary market and political cooperation among individual citizens.

Buchanan states that economic growth and social prosperity arise from the institutions that allow for voluntary exchange to take place, in the post-constitutional setting.

The lynchpin that binds citizen allegiance to obey the rule of law is future economic growth, in which all citizens have an equal opportunity to benefit.

In other words, the linkage between citizen allegiance to the rule of law in pre-constitutional fair rules and post-constitutional fair institutions is future economic growth. [a growing pie].

Peter J. Boettke and Christopher J. Coyne describe the relative importance between the function of economic growth, and economic re-distribution of wealth by the elites in government.

They state,

"The distribution of product among social classes [welfare redistribution] is clearly secondary to production…[economic growth]. [Economic growth occurs] by the removal of government constraints on individual liberty." (Boettke, Peter J. and Coyne, Christopher J., Methodological Individualism, Spontaneous Order and the Research Program of the Workshop in Political Theory and Policy Analysis, George Mason University, Department of Economics, 2004.).

We would add that the only fair method of dealing with the unequal wealth distribution, in the state of nature at the beginning of the pre-constitutional setting, is through future economic growth that opens the path for all citizens to become wealthy.

For example, in Madison's era, the unequal wealth of the 38 members of the ruling class who signed his document, would have eventually been remedied by economic growth, if his constitutional rules had not skewed the future distribution of benefits to his privileged natural aristocracy in the ensuing financial institutions of the shared plunder system of rewards.

Boettke and Coyne continue,

"[Buchanan's] main idea is that there are unintended consequences to purposeful human [market] action. These unintended consequences play a significant role in constituting the overall order [justice] of the system. As a result, what is needed is a set of [post-constitutional] institutions that allow individuals to act purposefully and make adjustments to the unintended consequences of those actions…The unintended consequences of those actions generate the social order… Social cooperation under the division of labor emerges when the norms and mores of a society support and reinforce the formal institutions of property and contract that enable the expansion of a market economy." (Boettke, Peter J., and Coyne, Christopher J., 2004.).

Buchanan states that the great moral virtue of the competitive free market system is that voluntary, cooperative social behavior coordination can be achieved without tyranny and totalitarianism to enforce citizen obedience to the rule of law.

The implementation of that voluntary, cooperative system though, depends on Buchanan's initial premise that individuals are rational and their own best guardians of individual welfare.

Buchanan states that,

"...for most persons, the independence offered by the presence of market alternatives offers the maximal liberty possible. But we have not yet designed institutions that will satisfy the individual's search for community in the impersonal setting of the market order without, at the same time, undermining the very independence that this order afford." (The Reason of Rules, 2008.).

In order for the emergence of stable social order to emerge, Buchanan argues that the power and unelected authority of the government must be limited to a specific set of tasks.

The point he makes is that a certain type of institutional judicial arrangement allows for the essential, primary function of government to enforce an equal application of the law, derived from rules that citizens give to themselves.

The teleos of the system of justice is to reduce the arbitrary and capricious application of the rules of justice by ruling class elites who escape the jurisdiction of the law.

The pre-constitutional rules would establish a priority of local and state governments over national governments, based on the principle that those bound most tightly by collective rules, must be given the greatest say in the making and enforcing of the rules.

This priority of local government over national government has a very subtle point about equality before the law. If all individuals are equal in the making and enforcing of the law, and the law is applied most stringently at the most local level of the community, then no individual is greater than the law.

In order to promote the greatest level of individual freedom, all individuals must be bound, in equal capacity, by the same law that they have given to themselves, at all levels of government.

The priority of local government is related to how local laws most directly affect the individual in his or her every day pursuit of sovereignty.

It is the local zoning law that commands a certain use of land, the local property tax that consumes income, and local occupational and business licensing laws that most immediately damage individual freedom gained in free market exchange.

Buchanan, like George Mason, would adopt a state-sovereignty framework of government that would limit the power of the central government.

We argue that the main source of unelected power in Madison's constitution arises from the function of the Federal Reserve Bank to manipulate money supply and interest rates to the benefit of private commercial banks and large corporations.

Hamilton implemented the First National Bank, in the post-constitutional setting, after Madison's constitution had been implemented in the fraudulent ratification process.

Boettke and Coyne write,

"The connection [Buchanan sees between free market exchange and individual liberty] begins with his individualistic approach to economics. Individuals have their own goals and desires, and the purpose of economic activity is to enable them to cooperate with each other so they can further those goals. As economists depict it, individuals have "utility functions" and they make choices that enable them to maximize their utility [wealth]. What this means in more common language is that individuals have their own goals, which each individual understands better than does anyone else. And the subject of economics, as Buchanan saw it, is to analyze how individuals interact for their mutual benefit in furtherance of those goals." Boettke, Peter J. and Coyne, Christopher J., 2004.).

In voluntary market exchange, individuals can opt out of transactions if they do not see the transactions as likely to further their interests.

A free market allows people to interact with each other for mutual gain and helps prevent common citizen exploitation by the ruling class.

As we noted in the previous chapter, both Mason and Buchanan identified reciprocal exchanges, and mutuality among citizens, as the foundation of democratic free society.

Buchanan's principle of free market exchange leaves each individual citizen free to pursue whatever is feasible within the limits of the legal or market institutional rules.

The case of opting out in the political market is different in the sense that individual citizens, acting through the authority of the state government, are the legal actors that can opt out of the existing unfair constitutional order.

The case of Brexit is an example of citizens in the U. K. opting out of an existing political contract.

Buchanan stated that politics is about finding peaceful agreements among people with different preferences on collective outcomes.

Politics, unlike science, is not about making "truth judgments" about fair and just economic or political outcomes, after economic exchanges have occurred.

The post-constitutional challenge is to discover the set of citizen participatory rules that best promote the making of political compromises among people with different preferences.

Individuals are observed to cooperate with one another, in the market, to reach agreements. Buchanan calls the network of relationships that emerges or evolves out of this trading process, "the market." (Buchanan, James M., and Tullock, Gordon, The Calculus of Consent: Logical Foundations of Constitutional Democracy, 1962.).

Buchanan defines the institutional market simply as a financial exchange forum for individual citizens. Unlike conventional macro-economic theory, Buchanan asserts that the market neither maximizes production efficiency nor minimizes unequal distributions of wealth and income.

The institutional market simply allows participants to pursue the goals which they value, subject to the preferences and endowments of others, and within the constraints of general "pre-constitutional rules of the game" that provide incentives for individuals to work and open enterprises.

The stable social order of the market emerges through the decisions of individuals to buy or sell or refrain from buying or selling.

The market process consists of voluntary decisions that create the pricing mechanism of supply and demand.

It is only through the process of the free market exchange that the price information is brought into existence and becomes a universal information asset in the economy.

It is exclusively the universality of prices throughout the market that allows for the emergence of a stable social order in the market economy.

Buchanan argues that automatic price adjustments are characterized by the organization of private decision-making in such a way that the desired monetary predictability will emerge from the ordinary operations of the economic system.

Our primary economic argument in favor of Buchanan's constitutional rules is that future price predictability and monetary stability occurs as a result of free market exchange, which leads to the emergence of stable social order.

In contrast, we argue that price and monetary stability, in the American economy, can never be achieved by financial elites at the Federal Reserve Bank because they are not as smart as the price-based market exchange outcomes derived by the Walrasian auctioneer.

Buchanan contends that the standard rule for the monetary policy of the nation is,

"Predictability in the value of the monetary unit, or, reciprocally, in the absolute level of prices." Importantly, this criterion [of future predictability] differs from monetary stability…monetary stability is plagued with vagueness. Predictability, especially with reference to the general level of prices, is free from that difficulty Furthermore, predictability, by maintaining "continuous monetary equilibrium" would entail real efficiency gains: by enshrining, in the form of a [binding constitutional] rule, the purchasing power of the monetary unit, economic actors would better be able to coordinate their activities, resulting in further exhaustion of the gains from trade than would otherwise exist… institutions of private [free market exchange] decision-making in such a way that the desired monetary predictability will emerge spontaneously from the ordinary operations of the system" (Buchanan, 1962.).

We agree with Buchanan's conclusion that,

"Unconstrained government monopoly in money creation cannot emerge from a genuine constitutional calculus, The argument for a monetary constitution is an argument for true rules, which actually bind monetary policy decision makers." (1962.).

Money, for Buchanan, offers no survival-enhancing capacity for citizens, and offers no sensory or aesthetic value.

In its most abstracted functional embodiment, money has value only because of its potential power to secure real value from others who will voluntarily take money in exchanges.

Money, for Buchanan, is simply, and exclusively, a medium of exchange in the market, not a store of value.

The standard of value for money, as a medium of exchange, is the rate of economic growth of the national gross domestic product, not some fixed value of a commodity, like bricks or gold.

Buchanan affirms that the rule for increasing the money supply must be constitutional.

"In application to money, the requirement is that the value of the monetary unit be made one of the rules of the game, within which economic interaction takes place, rather than being used as a counter in the strategy of play within the rules. In Hayekian parlance, the value of money must be part of the 'higher law,' as opposed to ordinary legislation that takes place within such law." (Buchanan, James M.,

The Limits of Liberty: Between Anarchy and Leviathan, University of Chicago Press, 1975.).

The elites at the Federal Reserve Bank, in manipulating the money supply, maximize their own social class welfare, and are incapable of maximizing social welfare because they do not have future price information to guide their decisions, even if they could argue that they were maximizing an imaginary social welfare function.

In the absence of future price information, the Fed runs up irresponsible future debts, and prints too much worthless paper currency, which causes macro-economic instability about every 10 years.

The ruling class escapes unharmed by the economic instability, but the middle and working class financial welfare is devastated by the economic instability caused by the Fed.

Boettke, et al., write,

"Fiscal deficits undermine the ability of monetary authorities to pursue an independent monetary policy course. When the federal government spends more than it takes in as revenue, the Treasury must finance the deficit by borrowing from the private sector in the form of government bonds. As government issues more bonds, the greater demand for loanable funds pushes interest rates up (Hein 1991). Monetary authorities often are under pressure to create conditions conducive to the issuance of new debt [shared plunder spoils] by offsetting the interest rate increases (Cochrane 2011a, b). Historically, such cases are not uncommon, occurring [about every 10 years] even in the United States following the Second World War." (2018.).

They argue that because of the linkage ensuring that budget debts will have future monetary effects, Fed monetary policy and fiscal debt are inseparable, under Madison's unlimited implied powers to grow the government.

Buchanan, like Adam Smith, understood that the costs of government projects funded with debt are passed on to the future generations who, as citizen-taxpayers, must repay the debt.

Although those future citizens who pay the interest and principle on future debt are worse off as a result of paying more in taxes or receiving less in government services, other citizens, today, who receive repayment of the debt [the ruling class] are better off by the same amount.

Buchanan concluded that it is not current period bondholders who are burdened with financing the expenditures, since they will be repaid in the future and they voluntarily choose to lend the money, indicating their decision that they are better off.

Instead, the future middle class taxpayer bears the burden of today's debt-financed expenditures.

Because Madison's rules contain no limits on the power of the government to limit debt or money creation, why would politicians, who benefit from shared plunder corruption, pay attention to common citizens who are not yet born?

In his theory of fiscal choice, Buchanan sought to explain government spending and taxing decisions as arising from the same profit motives that economists assume guide spending and consumption decisions of individuals in private market exchanges.

Because the Fed is a private bank, it is not bound any pre-constitutional rules in Madison's rules on increasing the money supply or funding government debt.

If the Fed has the unlimited discretion to follow its own rules that benefit the ruling class, then what exists in America, according to Buchanan, is unlimited monetary discretion, which is constitutionally unjustifiable. (Brennan and Buchanan 1981.).

Buchanan asserts that no legal mechanism binds the hands of the Fed's discretion, or punishes monetary authorities for deviating from the interest rate prices given in free market exchange.

Boettke notes that,

"As long as the [monetary] rule is clear and binding, a true monetary rule meets Buchanan's predictability requirement. Buchanan probably would prefer predictability specifically in the form of stabilizing money's purchasing power, which fits most neatly with some form of price level targeting or inflation targeting. The most important criterion is whether the rule actually binds, [the discretionary power] and thus serves as a foundation for market actors to form reliable expectations about the future." (2018.).

Buchanan argues that future price predictability and monetary stability does not require a central bank or central monetary authority to either manage the monetary base or execute a monetary rule using discretion on setting short term interest rates.

Buchanan defines the acceptable limits of authority of the centralized government into two broad functions, which he calls "the protective state," and "the productive state."

As Buchanan defines it, the productive state arises from an agreement among citizens to pool their resources to collectively produce goods and services that would be difficult to produce individually or through standard market activity.

These collective goods may include national defense and border protection from invasion, or an internal transportation system.

In the development of pre-constitutional rules, the provision of collective goods must be "expressly" delegated by citizens to the central government, in an act of consent of the governed.

Buchanan writes that,

"The protective state emerges as the enforcing agency or institution, conceptually external to the contracting parties. In this capacity, the state is external to contracting parties [in market exchange] and does not "produce" anything other than contract enforcement. The productive state, on the other hand, produces collective goods. These two roles of the state are conceptually distinct, and the failure to distinguish these roles leads to confusion. For example, the law is a form of "public capital" that emerges from an initial anarchistic equilibrium as part of "an all-inclusive legal contract for the whole community" (Buchanan, James M., The Limits of Liberty: Between Anarchy and Leviathan, University of Chicago Press, 1977.).

We contrast the relative macro-economic stability under the era of free banking, between 1840 and 1913, with the real bills money doctrine, of Fed's manipulation, under the various eras of the central national bank.

The economic stability in the free banking era occurred under cooperation between various private state banks.

Inter-bank market transactions in the free banking era were carried out using bank liabilities as the medium of exchange. Payment for commodities typically changed hands only when banks cleared their liabilities against each other.

It was in a bank's private self-interest to accept competitor bank notes at par, which then required a system for exchanging each other's liabilities to ascertain net commodity clearings.

Eventually, the practice of multilateral clearing served as a crucial locus of self-governance among private banks.

Clearinghouses monitored banks for fraud, maintained quality controls, such as minimum capital requirements, and sometimes even performed functions similar to those recommended by last-resort lending theory. Clearinghouses thus served as a successful example of private and voluntary governance in the era before central banks. (Timberlake, Richard H., The Central Banking Role of Clearinghouse Associations, Journal of Money, Credit and Banking, 1984.).

Timberlake notes that,

"The reason the free banking systems between 1840 and 1913, promoted macroeconomic stability is simple: banks had a financial incentive to meet changes in money demand with corresponding changes in money supply. Suppose that the demand for money rises. Banks would notice their commodity reserves gradually increasing, which would signal to them they could profitably issue more liabilities and use those liabilities to purchase new assets. Since market actors use bank liabilities as money, such actions in effect increase the money supply."

In applying Buchanan's individual rights constitutional rules for maximum social prosperity to Mason's ideology of individual liberty, the pre-constitutional rules would expressly curtail the ability of post-constitutional institutions to change the rules of the game, after the new constitution had been ratified, by the consent of the governed.

Monetary policy, tax systems, tax rates, and limits on government spending and debt, would all be included as components under the pre-constitutional setting.

In the post-constitutional institutional setting, the agencies of the national government, and elected representatives, would be bound by rules on increasing taxation linked to clear sources of revenue, to tax systems with uniform rates on the allowed tax bases, and ideally to tax bases that are complementary to the public services desired.

In that constitutional framework, the Congressional justification for the authority of the Fed, and the discretionary authority of the Fed to manipulate money supply and interest rates would be eliminated.

Buchanan cites the freedom of citizens to opt out of free market exchanges as a great virtue of the market system of prices. Citizens who do not want to buy a product are not coerced by agents of government to buy the product.

The freedom of citizens in the market provides price signals in the macro supply and demand relationships which guide future economic growth.

Buchanan notes that, just as individuals are free to trade in markets for their mutual benefit, citizens can also engage in political exchange for the benefit of everyone in the voting system.

Buchanan cites the right of secession for citizens to withdraw from the existing constitution as analogous to the freedom of citizens not to buy a product in free market exchange.

Boettke notes,

"To this end, he recommends the possibility of secession. If lower-level governments have the right to secede from the jurisdiction of a higher-level government, the higher-level government has stronger incentives to govern wisely and effectively than if secession were impossible. The United States was formed in this way when the colonies seceded from Great Britain. More recently, and similarly, Great Britain seceded from the European Union."

The conflict over a state's right of secession is a legal red-herring, and Buchanan got that part of his theory wrong.

Following Buchanan's and Mason's individualist ideology, it is not states that have the right of secession, it is individual citizens who may opt out of an unfair constitutional contract, in the same way that citizens opt out of unfair market contracts.

The issue of citizen sovereignty, mutuality, and reciprocity among citizens will continue under a new constitution that severely limits the undelegated power of the central government.

We argue that in Madison's initial statement, "We, the people," means individual citizens, not states, formed Madison's constitution.

And in perfect logical symmetry if "We, the people," created the constitution, then the right of replacing the existing constitution remains with "We, the people," not "We, the states."

We cite the authority of this interpretation by Supreme Court Justice Thomas, in his dissent in the Term Limits case.

As cited by Daniel Farber, in The Fourteenth Amendment and the Unconstitutionality of Secession, (Farber, Daniel A., Akron Law Review, 2015).

"Justice Thomas invoked a similar conception of federalism. In his Term Limits dissent, he said that the "ultimate source of the Constitution's authority is the consent of the people of each individual State, not the consent of the undifferentiated people of the Nation as a whole," adding that "the people of the several States are the only true source of power." He seemed to indicate state sovereignty remains primary today: "the people of each State retained their separate political identities," and the "very name 'congress' suggests a coming together of representatives from distinct entities."

Under the Articles of Confederation, Farber notes, states would continue to possess the right of secession.

Farber writes,

"The right to secede is a natural feature of a confederation where citizens owe allegiance to their own individual local governments, but out of place in a nation that demands the primary allegiance of its citizens and in turn promises to protect their rights from interference by local governments."

The fundamental legal conflict over where ultimate sovereignty resides between Madison and Mason, is that Madison's concept of sovereignty is the central government, as a collective legal entity.

Mason's concept of sovereignty resides in individual citizens who agree to form a new government when they leave the state of nature.

King George surrendered the sovereignty of his Crown, to the individual citizens who resided in the 13 sovereign states.

Prior to the King's surrender, British citizens owned their allegiance to the sovereignty of the Crown.

After the surrender, sovereignty was transferred by the King to individual citizens of the respective states, codified in the Articles of Confederation.

Madison shifted the sovereignty of American citizens to the sovereignty of the national government, but cited the sovereignty of "We, the people," as his authority to overthrow the Articles.

U. S. Supreme Court decisions about the unlimited implied powers of the central government cite the third Article in the Articles of Confederation about perpetual union of friendship among states, as if that precedent is legal justification for Madison's perpetual constitution.

The third article of the Articles of Confederation states:

"The better to secure and perpetuate mutual friendship and intercourse among the people of the different states in this union, the free inhabitants of each of these states, paupers, vagabonds and fugitives from Justice excepted, shall be entitled to all privileges and immunities of free citizens in the several states…"

The citation to the prior authority of the Articles is legally and constitutionally, invalid. As a delegate said during the Constitutional Convention of 1787, that prior document was "unknown" to Madison's document.

Madison's Preamble used a linguistic ruse [We, the people] that the individual citizens were sovereign, just as citizens were sovereign under Mason's principle that all legitimate authority of government is derived from the consent of the governed.

Farber cites the Supreme Court decision in Corfield v. Coryell (1823), which is based upon Mason's definition of rights in his Virginia Declaration of Rights.

Farber writes, that in the Corfield decision,

"The Comity Clause protected "those privileges and immunities which are, in their nature, fundamental; which belong, of right, to the citizens of all free governments; and which have, at all times, been enjoyed by the citizens of the several states."Among these rights were "[p]rotection by the government; the enjoyment of life and liberty, with the right to acquire and possess property of every kind, and to pursue and obtain happiness and safety; subject nevertheless to such restraints as the government may justly prescribe for the general good of the whole."

Consequently, in Madison's rules, the 13 states, as legal entities, ceded their sovereignty to the all-powerful central government, but individual citizens never ceded their sovereignty, and their individual liberty does not depend on where they reside, because citizen sovereignty is not defined by geographical territory.

Individual liberty, as noted by both Mason and Jefferson, is derived from God. Natural rights inure to individual citizens, not to legal entities such as large corporations, states or the national government.

Buchanan is correct in his assertion that citizens have a right to opt out of Madison's unfair rules, which were ratified in a fraudulent, illegitimate ratification process, and were never ratified by "We, the people."

There is no legal or moral principle in American constitutional history that compels citizens to remain in an oppressive, tyrannical, regime, against their will.

Buchanan's rules link the individual choice, in the free market system, to individual choice in the political system because economic individualism is linked to equal political natural rights.

No other constitutional configuration starts out with this set of equal natural rights, aiming at the social goal to create "maximum" individual happiness. Equal natural rights create maximum economic growth, which, in turn, creates maximum social welfare.

The relationship between constitutional individual freedom and national economic growth is through the ability of individuals to create new technology ventures that commercialize new technology products.

Nations which have constitutional rules that aim at individual freedom and happiness have the greatest rates of economic growth and upward occupational mobility.

New products and new markets may emerge, given a specific configuration of cultural values and laws that favor individual initiative and the appropriation of rewards based upon individual merit

Unless the citizens agree, at the very beginning of the nation, in pre-constitutional rules to create constitutional limits on the corruption of the elites, the national economy will not grow.

The economy will cycle endlessly through the empirically observed boom bust performance generated by the Fed's manipulation of the money supply for the benefit of banks and large corporations.

We argue that there is only one legitimate configuration of Buchanan's constitutional rules, and only one method of citizen participation, of providing consent, in the making of fair constitutional rules, that creates maximum rates of economic growth, and maximum diffusion of income benefits of economic growth to all social classes of citizens.

In Buchanan's conception of the new constitution, if citizens in the pre-constitutional setting decide to allow either citizens, or states, to opt out of the post-constitutional rules, that right would be a guaranteed constitutional right, just as it was in the Confederation.

Chapter 6. The Evolutionary Entrepreneurial Capitalist Economy of Joseph Schumpeter.

Schumpeter's entrepreneurial capitalism is based upon the individual initiative of a single person who has the drive and insight to create new products and new ventures.

Schumpeter's economic theory of individual liberty, just like Mason's political theory and Buchanan's constitutional theories, is based upon the ideology of individual freedom to prosper through free market exchange.

Schumpeter contrasts evolutionary entrepreneurial capitalism with another form of capitalism, called crony corporate global capitalism.

He writes,

"The essential point to grasp is that in dealing with [entrepreneurial] capitalism we are dealing with an evolutionary process … Capitalism, then, is by nature a form or method of economic change and not only never is but never can be stationary … The fundamental new impulse that sets and keeps the capitalist engine in motion comes from the new consumers' goods, the new methods of production or transportation, the new markets, the new forms of industrial organization that capitalist enterprise creates … the same process of industrial mutation … that incessantly revolutionizes the economic structure from within, incessantly destroying the old one, incessantly creating a new one. This process of Creative Destruction is the essential fact about capitalism. It is what capitalism consists in and what every capitalist concern has got to live in … Every piece of business strategy acquires its true significance only against the background of that process and within the situation created by it." (Schumpeter, Joseph, A., Capitalism, Socialism, and Democracy, Harper Perennial, 1962.).

We argue that Schumpeter's entrepreneurial economic theory is consistent with the constitutional framework of James Buchanan, and we place Schumpeter's theory into the Buchanan individualist framework to derive economic principles for a new constitution.

In contrast, Madison's theory of government is based upon the British social class conflict model, which is more compatible with the group collectivist philosophy of the Marxist theory of social class exploitation.

In Jefferson's Declaration of Independence, he explained that the break with the King represented an entirely new concept of society based upon the free economic independence of common yeoman farmers.

Today, Jefferson's faith in the independent small farmer economy would be called entrepreneurial capitalism, where all citizens have an equal opportunity to achieve happiness and prosperity through individual initiative.

In entrepreneurial capitalism, the profits from entrepreneurial capital investments are re-invested through decisions by individual entrepreneurs seeking future prosperity, in Buchanan's free market exchange institutions.

The ability of an entrepreneur to re-invest the first generation of profits into a second generation of ventures is the most important dynamic of free market economic growth.

As Schumpeter notes in, The Economics and Sociology of Capitalism,

"Entrepreneurial profit proper… arises in the capitalist economy wherever a new method of production, a new commercial combination, or a new form or organization is successfully introduced. It is the premium which capitalism attaches to innovation … If this profit were taxed away, that element of the economic process would be lacking which at present is by far the most important individual motive for work toward industrial progress. Even if taxation merely reduced this profit substantially, industrial development would process considerably more slowly, as the fate of Austria plainly shows … there is a limit to the taxation of entrepreneurial profit beyond which tax pressure cannot go without first damaging and then destroying the tax object." (Schumpeter, Joseph A. The Economics and Sociology of Capitalism, Nee, Victor, and Swedberg, Richard, eds. Princeton University Press. 1991.).

The major point Schumpeter is making about entrepreneurial profits is that the re-investment of profits, by the entrepreneur, is the most critical factor in causing future economic growth, and is also the cause of the evolutionary pattern of economic development in a market exchange economy.

Schumpeter makes a distinction between entrepreneurial capitalism, which evolves through different economic epochs, and the large global crony corporate economy, based upon maintenance of the status quo political and financial advantages of the ruling class, which seeks a return to a former equilibrium, after a disturbance.

In making the distinction between small entrepreneurial firms and large corporations, Schumpeter identifies the key advantage that Hamilton's central banking system obtains for the ruling class in Madison's constitution framework.

Schumpeter writes,

"Capitalism is that form of private property economy in which innovations are carried out by means of borrowed money, which in general, though not by logical necessity, implies credit creation. Bank loans supply the venture capital." (Schumpeter, Joseph A., Business Cycles: A Theoretical, Historical, and Statistical Analysis of the Capitalist Process, McGraw-Hill Book Company. 1939.).

In other words, the undelegated political power of Hamilton's central bank controls the capitalist economy through their ability to control credit and the banking system for entrepreneurs and small business owners.

This unelected, undelegated power of the Fed is exercised through the manipulation of money supply and interest rates, which is the exclusive domain of the Federal Reserve Bank, in Hamilton's financial system.

In pre-constitutional rule making, Madison established the unchecked power of the ruling class to make all social and political decisions, and in the post-constitutional setting, Hamilton's central bank created the institutional framework of unchecked private banking power for banks.

The two parts of Madison's rules work together, in tandem, to create a wildly erratic economy, to the financial detriment of common citizens and small business.

Schumpeter noted that Madison's rules had already been well-established, by the mid-1930s, and were working well for the ruling class, in America.

Schumpeter wrote,

"Government control of the capital and labour markets, of price policies and, by means of taxation, of income redistribution is already established and needs only to be complemented systematically by government initiative in indicating the general lines of production (housing programs, foreign investment) in order to transform, even without extensive nationalization of industries, regulated, or fettered, capitalism into a guided capitalism that might, with almost equal justice, be called socialism. Thus, the prediction of whether the capitalist order will survive is, in part, a matter of terminology." (Schumpeter, Joseph A., Essays On Entrepreneurs, Innovations, Business Cycles and the Evolution of Capitalism, Clemence, Richard V., ed., Routledge, 1989.).

We agree with Schumpeter that crony global capitalism is well established, under the authority of Madison's flawed constitution, and that that form of capitalism must be replaced by entrepreneurial capitalism.

In The Sociology of Imperialisms, Schumpeter makes the assertion that small business foots the bill for the power of the banks and big business pockets the profits.

Schumpeter writes,

"The policies of high finance are based on the control of a *large* proportion of the national capital, but they are in the actual [financial] interest of only a *small* proportion [of the ruling class]. Schumpeter, Joseph A. "The Sociology of Imperialisms." in, Schumpeter, Joseph A., Imperialism and Social Classes. Paul M. Sweezy, ed., Blackwell, 1951.).

In his 1910 analysis of the American banking system, Rudolf Hilferding writes,

"The banks skew credit towards large firms and away from small productive [firms], a loan to a [large] corporation is easier to police. The banks hold similar blocs of shares and send their delegates to the same boards of directors: involved in common projects, they are in a strong position to promote cartels and encourage amalgamation. The banks themselves regard each other as legitimate takeover targets. In this way, the tendency of both bank capital and industrial capital to eliminate competition coincides." (Hilferding, Rudolf, Finance Capital. A Study of the Latest

Phase of Capitalist Development. Bottomore, Tom, ed., Routledge, 1981.).

In the absence of the dynamic of individual initiative over profit re-investment, the ruling class control of the monetary system and capital investment, leads to an erratic boom-bust economy.

Schumpeter writes,

"[The reason]why central planned economies fail is because it cannot utilize either the knowledge of opportunities or the incentive structures that emerge naturally in markets...because [free] markets exploit the forces of competiton." (Buchanan, James A., Economic Freedom and Federalism: Prospect for a New Century, The Collected Works of James Buchanan, The Liberty Fund, 2001.).

For example, the reason why communist China's economy is doomed to failure is because individual entrepreneurs cannot appropriate the reward of the future profit from their initiative to create new ventures.

In the absence of individual entrepreneurial re-investment from past profits, the Chinese economy cannot grow.

The only way the Chinese communist collectivist economy can grow is by stealing technology innovation from U. S. firms, and replicating the technology by government-directed investments in Chinese champion industries.

When the Chinese can no longer steal U. S. technology, their economic growth will stop.

The profit of an entrepreneur is mal-appropriated by the Communist government.

Schumpeter addresses the malappropriation of the profits, by the government in China, and the similar malappropriation, by the national government in America, by high taxes.

Specifically regarding the taxation of entrepreneurial profit, Schumpeter writes,

"If this [entrepreneurial] profit were taxed away, that element of the economic process [economic growth] would be lacking which at present is by far the most important individual motive for work toward industrial progress. Even if taxation merely reduced this profit substantially, industrial development would progress considerably more slowly ... there is a limit to the taxation of entrepreneurial profit beyond which tax pressure cannot go without first damaging and then destroying the tax object. (Schumpeter,

Joseph A., The Economics and Sociology of Capitalism. Swedberg, Richard, ed., Princeton University Press, 1991).

The mal-appropriation of profits by the Chinese elites, and the subsequent re-deployment of profits in capital investments directed by the elites, short-circuits Schumpeter's theory of future economic growth obtained in free market entrepreneurial investments.

The reason why the U. S. economy is subject to periodic boom-bust cycles is that the majority of private capital investment decisions are made by a tiny group of banking and corporate elites, just as it is in China.

The major incentive to invest in both societies is to reward members of the banking and political ruling class, not to create sustained future economic growth that benefits common citizens.

The profits from the asset speculation of the American elites are not shared widely through the free market income and employment multiplier effects, which distribute benefits of economic growth to the social classes in society.

The asset speculation in real estate and stocks is caused by the Fed's manipulation of the money supply and interest rates, which are aimed at improving the welfare of the ruling class, creating the mirage of economic growth. [real bills doctrine].

Absent entrepreneurial economic growth in the American economy, what remains would be perpetual imitation of technology innovation, as is the case with China's economy, causing the economy to ratchet down to a lower level of aggregate demand.

According to Schumpeter, technology innovations are essential to explaining economic growth, and the "entrepreneur" is the central innovator.

As Schumpeter described in The Theory of Economic Development the entrepreneur's main function is to allocate existing resources to "new uses and new combinations".

One of Schumpeter's most lasting contributions was his insight that entrepreneurship is at once a unique factor of production, in the current time period, and the rare social input, in the future time period, which makes economic evolution proceed to the next epoch.

Our economic argument is not that the rates of American economic growth are non-existent. Economic growth in the American economy is a mirage. It is erratic, transitory and temporary.

Rather, our argument is that Schumpeter's entrepreneurial economy, based upon free market private sector entrepreneurial investments, would lead to much greater rates of economic growth, whose benefits would be widely distributed to all American social classes.

Beyond the benefits of greater rates of future economic growth, and wider distribution of the income benefits of economic growth, the great virtue of Schumpeter's entrepreneurial economic theory is that it leads to the emergence of a stable political and economic order.

Schumpeter identifies entrepreneurial capital investment in technology innovation as the most important investments for promoting economic development.

Schumpeter writes,

"Technological breakthroughs are the very essence of capitalistic enterprise and hence cannot be divorced from it." (Schumpeter, Joseph A., Business Cycles: A Theoretical, Historical, and Statistical Analysis of the Capitalist Process, McGraw-Hill Book Company, 1939.).

Technology, as described by Schumpeter, means more than improvements in production efficiency in machinery and the chemicals inputs alone, in the current time period.

Schumpeter continues:

"To produce means to combine material and forces within our reach ... To produce other things, or the same things by a different method, means to combine these materials and forces differently. [production efficiency].In so far as the "new combination" may in time grow out of the old by continuous adjustment in small steps, there is certainly change, possibly growth, by neither a new phenomenon nor development in our sense. In so far as this is not the case, and the new combinations appear discontinuously, then the phenomenon characterizing development emerges. For reasons of expository convenience, henceforth, we shall only mean the latter case when we speak of new combinations of productive means. Development in our sense is then defined by the carrying out of new combinations." (Theory of Economic Development.).

Schumpeter's use of the term "technology innovation," encompasses the entire social structure and economic organization of the economy.

In other words, Schumpeter's use of the term technology innovation encompasses Buchanan's future post-constitutional financial and economic institutions which are created after the pre-constitutional rules have been established.

Schumpeter's theory of evolutionary entrepreneurial capitalism generates stable social order by eliminating the initial status quo current distribution of wealth, at the beginning of any 10-year boom-bust economic cycle.

Schumpeter's theory of capital investments predicts the creation of entirely new future markets, the creation of which bind the allegiance of citizens to obey the rule of law because they hope to prosper in the future economy.

As long as all citizens can see that they have a chance to prosper under fair constitutional rules, they extend the benefits of obeying the rule of law to all other citizens. [Mason's egalitarianism].

Schumpeter explains that the new future economy is dramatically different than the old economy.

He writes,

"The "new" economy is dramatically different from the old one that it has replaced. And, then, the process begins anew [from re-investment of entrepreneurial profit] . . .To begin with, increases in the quantity of money [by the Fed] never occur [never benefit] uniformly for all people. Further, people are never completely aware of the nature of the process, so that, at least for some time, they act as if they received higher incomes, [the mirage of economic growth] when the sum of [real] incomes remains constant. For both reasons, prices never rise uniformly – neither the prices for consumer goods relative to each other nor the prices of consumer goods relative to those of the means of production. Thereby the price rise ceases to be merely nominal. It means a real shift of wealth on the market for consumer goods and a real shift of power on the market for the means of production, and it affects the quantities of commodities and the whole productive process. No doubt, not all these effects are permanent … But very frequently such reestablishment of the [ruling class] status quo [in an entrepreneurial economy] is impossible. Newly-won positions may be permanently held, and old ones permanently lost, and much in the life of the economy may thereby change – as forms of business organization, direction and methods of production, etc." (Schumpeter, Joseph A., The Theory of Economic Development, Harvard University Press, 1934.).

To quote Adam Smith again, about the emergence of a stable social order,

"Every man, as long as he does not violate the laws of justice, is left perfectly free to pursue his own interest in his own way, and to bring both his industry and capital into competition with those of any other man, or order of men." (Smith, Adam. The Wealth of Nations, 1776.).

Schumpeter's entrepreneurial system of natural liberty clearly encompasses Buchanan's free market exchange, and prohibits economic exploitation and coercion of the ruling class over common citizens.

In The Justice of Natural Liberty, Buchanan quotes this passage from Adam Smith, and adds,

"To hurt in any degree the interest of any one order of [common] citizens for no other purpose but to promote that of some other [ruling class], is evidently contrary to that justice and equality of treatment which the sovereign owes to all different orders of his subjects… Markets are grounded ethically in the fundamental principle of justice that declares that people should deal with each other through cooperative action rather than by [coercive] force. (Buchanan, 1976.).

Buchanan's fair constitutional rules link individual choice, in the free market exchange system, to individual choice in the political exchange system.

Schumpeter adds the theoretical justification of individual liberty by attaching the imperative of future economic growth to the creation of a stable social order.

We argue that the greatest rates of future economic growth occur under conditions of entrepreneurial capitalism.

The relationship between constitutional individual freedom and national economic growth is through the ability of individuals to create new technology ventures that commercialize new technology products.

New products and new markets may emerge, given a specific configuration of constitutional laws and financial institutions, which favor individual initiative and the individual appropriation of future rewards, based upon individual merit.

In such a society, the appearance of technical progress is rapidly diffused, and as the new knowledge is embodied in new ventures, the technology spreads throughout the economy, creating imbalances and bottlenecks in existing interindustry supply chain relations.

In entrepreneurial parlance, these imbalances and bottlenecks in the former supply chains create entrepreneurial private capital investment opportunities.

Filling the supply chain gaps for the new ventures and new interindustry supply chains, creates entirely new future industrial and consumer markets.

The emergence of those new future markets is commonly called "economic growth," and it is the future economic growth which allows a stable social order to emerge because all citizens want a fair opportunity to prosper under their common allegiance to obey the rule of law. [Work hard. Play by the rules].

Once a successful technology innovation has been made, Schumpeter states that,

"A swarm of entrepreneurs emerge and eventually a whole [evolutionary] business cycle is set in motion."

The fairness of Buchanan's constitutional rules is connected to Schumpeter's imperative of future economic growth, derived in an entrepreneurial capitalist society.

The right kind of cultural and social values for an entrepreneurial economy to thrive only occur under a specific set of pre-constitutional rules and post-constitutional financial institutions that are based upon individual liberty as the mission of the new nation.

As Joel Mokyr states, in The Lever of Riches: Technological Creativity and Economic Progress,

"For technological progress to occur, it must be born into a socially sympathetic environment." (Oxford University Press, 1990.).

According to Mokyr, economic growth results from open flows of technological knowledge, which only occur under one configuration of constitutional rules and cultural values.

Mokyr states that technological progress tends to occur in national economies which have well-educated citizens, who are deeply engaged in the economic and political decisions of their communities.

Mokyr suggests that there is an empirically observable sequence of events which occur in an economy that promotes technological innovation.

He writes,

"The causal chain could thus run from technological success to [new future distributions of] income and from there, to institutional change, rather than from institutional change to technological change." (The Lever of Riches.)

We argue that, if the future income distribution does not change, from the initial ruling class status quo distribution, then technological evolution will stagnate, which causes future economic growth to stagnate at some lower level of macro-economic aggregate demand.

In the absence of future economic growth, common citizens lose their allegiance to obey the rule of law because investment opportunities for common citizens are eliminated in the boom-bust recession.

This loss of allegiance to obey the rule of law is exacerbated when common citizens see the two-tiered justice system where ruling class elites do not obey the rule of law, and escape unharmed by the economic downturn.

Mokyr identifies the political forces in the American society which resist changes to the status quo distribution of income, and suggests that the social and political forces that resist a change in income distribution are more powerful [global corporations and banks] than the forces that promote technological innovation and sustained economic growth.

In America, today, there is no middle class or working class political ideology that is organized to promote the individualist, entrepreneurial economy.

In America, in 1787, there was no political middle class or working class ideology to counter Madison's and Hamilton's ruling class agenda in Madison's constitution.

Mokyr writes,

"Technological progress has run into an even more powerful foe: the purposeful self-interested resistance to new technology...Without an understanding of the political economy of technological change, then, the historical development of economic growth will remain a mystery."

Mokyr found, in his historical review of the causes of economic growth, that certain political organizations and social groups are opposed to open knowledge flows because that type of investment in technical change would tend to disrupt the advantages they receive from the existing status quo arrangement of power. (Mokyr, Joel, The Gifts of Athena: Historical Origins of the Knowledge Economy, Princeton University Press, 2002.).

Charles Kindleberger, in World Economic Primacy, noted how a certain set of cultural values tended to favor an attitude towards technical innovation. He characterized this attitude as,

"The capability and will of individuals, companies and governments to break free of existing habits, perceptions, institutions, and task allocations, in order to revise them in light of constantly changing circumstances and developments." (Kindleberger, Charles P., World Economic Primacy: 1500-1990, Oxford University Press, 1996.).

Like Mokyr, Buchanan and Schumpeter, Kindleberger also perceived a type of contingent relationship between the cultural values and constitutional rules that support individual freedom and national economic growth.

He found that individuals in some societies have the freedom to break free of existing habits, perceptions, and institutions in order to revise their behavior in light of changing economic conditions and future economic uncertainty.

In other societies, Kindleberger found a type of economic control exercised over individuals that inhibited changed behavior.

Some political organizations with a vested financial interest in maintaining the status quo arrangement of power tended to oppose technical change, and thus act to limit individual economic freedom, in order to control the pace and direction of economic growth.

Both Mokyr and Kindleberger attach moral importance to economic growth that results from technological change. In other words, both writers tend to make a moral judgment that technical change that creates economic growth is a desired pre-constitutional end for society.

Mokyr and Kindleberger attach moral importance to future economic growth because the future growth emphasizes individual entrepreneurial freedom, and the prospect of greater individual incomes for all social classes.

Richard Florida, in The Distinct Personality of Entrepreneurial Cities, explains the connection between the entrepreneurial culture and tacit knowledge creation.

Florida states,

"The entrepreneurial culture (an environment that fosters entrepreneurship) creates an economy where entrepreneurs have the drive and resilience to overcome obstacles, are more open to new ideas, and are able to connect with people, build and lead teams, and get things done… The entrepreneurial culture interacts with and connects to local (tacit) knowledge and talent. As Renfrow puts it, "new knowledge will have a greater propensity to generate entrepreneurship in regions with a pronounced entrepreneurial culture where the predominant attitudes and norms reinforce individual's decisions to act upon entrepreneurial opportunities." (Bloomberg News, August 3, 2015.).

Technological investments that promote economic growth according to Moykr and Kindelberger, are a "public" good to be aimed at as a constitutional goal for societies that value greater individual incomes.

Florida adds the proviso that the entrepreneurial culture only occurs in a specific cultural and institutional configuration, primarily in metro regions.

Their language of economic growth as a "public good," is consistent with Buchanan's characterization of the function of government as the "productive state."

In the productive state, government rules about technical innovation lead to economic growth, which then contributes to individual freedom, because citizens have a common allegiance to obey the rule of law.

Buchanan agrees with Moykr and Kindelberger about the moral importance of economic growth by stating that free market exchange, based upon the price mechanism, will lead society, automatically, to a stable society.

As applied to technical progress, in Madison's collectivist class conflict model, technological progress is controlled by large corporations, in alliance with government funding, which leads to centralized research and development, primarily in American universities, and independent research labs, like the one in Wuhan.

This globalist corporate orientation is weak in its ability to spin out new entrepreneurial ventures because, under the authority of the Fed, global crony corporatism controls investment decisions about new technological ventures. [BioNTech].

Opening up investment opportunities for common citizens to obtain entrepreneurial individual wealth is not highly regarded as a mission of the nation, in Madison's British social class conflict model.

In the crony corporate globalist form of capitalism, it is not inadequate economic adaptation of the old firms, to the new technology, that halts American economic growth.

Rather, it is crony capitalist political manipulation of the government rules and creation of money that causes inflation, when the old firms try to use political power to maintain the status quo distribution of income.

The crony capitalist political manipulation of government agents and elected representatives benefits the status quo ruling class, of so-called "old money."

Buchanan's faith in common citizens to make fair rules under the veil of uncertain futures, gives way, in Madison's rules, to a priority on maintaining the status quo distribution of income, under a centralized, collectivist political system, that is disconnected entirely from the consent of the governed.

In other words, in the absence of fair constitutional rules, the American society gives way to Madison's cultural value of ruling class shared plunder, enabled by the manipulation of money and interest rates, by the Fed.

Schumpeter argued that the analysis of economic growth should be focused on a dynamic historical perspective that incorporated a maco theory of social change.

In addressing what economists should do, in their professional lives, he wrote,

"The focus of our analytical attention is to be a dynamic theory of social change, then we must have agents of social change. Unless we fail to focus on these agents of change and instead concentrate on social forces beyond the individual's control, then we will not be able to develop a theory of social change." (Schumpeter, Joseph A., The Economics and Sociology of Capitalism, Princeton University Press, 1991.).

Schumpeter identifies a type of cancel culture in crony corporatism that resists new ideas and potential changes to the status quo of income distribution.

Schumpeter writes,

"Any deviating conduct by a member of a social group is condemned, though in greatly varying degrees according as the social group is used to such conduct or not. Even a deviation from social custom in such things as dress or manner arouses opposition, and of course all the more so in the graver cases." (The Economics and Sociology of Capitalism.).

The agent of change in Schumpeter's theory of social change is the entrepreneur.

The social forces in America which resist social change are the organized political forces of large global corporations and banks, such as the Business Roundtable, the US-China Business Council, and U. S. Chamber of Commerce, who work in partnership with the U. S. Congress, the agents of government and the Fed to maintain the existing status quo of income and wealth distribution.

In the Mason/Buchanan/Schumpeter entrepreneurial economy, social institutions are characterized by economic conditions that are in flux and ever changing.

In addition, in the entrepreneurial economy, few barriers exist to inhibit those who possess an entrepreneurial spirit to create a new venture.

Schumpeter described the forces of change in the entrepreneurial capitalist economy as akin to the gales of creative destruction.

Especially in a competitive market exchange economy the new technology innovation means the competitive elimination of the old social and economic order.

According to Raymond March,

"The Schumpeterian entrepreneur is a disruptive innovator that displaces existing business practices in a process of "creative destruction." (March, Raymond J., The Substance of Entrepreneurship and the Entrepreneurship of Substances, et al., SSRN, 2016.).

Schumpeter believed that entrepreneurship tended to emerge from a particular sort of person who possesses characteristics that could be described as an "entrepreneur-spirit."

Individuals with an entrepreneurial spirit have the ability to imagine the future and envision investment opportunities that others do not perceive. In imagining the future, the entrepreneurs are creating the new future markets by imagining how the future economy would operate.

Schumpeter writes,

"But whatever the type, everyone is an entrepreneur only when he actually "carries out new combinations,...He 'leads' the means of production into new channels. But this he does not by convincing people of the desirability of carrying out his plan or creating confidence in his leading in the manner of a political leader – the only man he has to convince or to impress is the banker who is to finance him." (Theory of Economic Development.).

Schumpeter characterizes the role of the entrepreneur in terms of knowledge creation and knowledge diffusion, through the price system.

Schumpeter writes,

Central to this understanding of the competitive market is the role of the entrepreneur. Through his pursuit of profit opportunities, the knowledge that is dispersed through the price system is discovered, utilized, and communicated to others, driving the market toward coordination. In this way, the most willing suppliers and the most willing demanders of any particular good or service are guided to realize the mutual gains from exchange in the least costly way. It is often cited that the source of "market failure" is in the difficulty of identifying external costs and benefits. However, it is from these so-called "inefficiencies" that the entrepreneur emerges in the pursuit of pure profit to mitigate these third-party effects."(Theory of Economic Development.).

For Schumpeter, entrepreneurial activity is not modeled as a discovery that exists "out there in the existing means of production." Entrepreneurship creates a new future reality based upon the discovery of new technological knowledge.

The creation of new technical knowledge is a social phenomenon caused by the interaction of humans engaged in social/business relationships, or as Buchanan would say, in the post-constitutional institutions of the market exchange economy.

Rinaldo Evangelista, explains, in Knowledge and Investment: The Sources of Innovation In Industry,

"The general process of technological change can be conceptualized as a process of generation of new technological knowledge as distinct from the process which leads to its actual use in production...in the form of new or improved machines, technical devices and operating systems." (Evangelista, Rinaldo, Knowledge and Investment: The Sources of Innovation in Industry, Edward Elgar Publishing, 1999.).

In this depiction of knowledge creation, the scientists, engineers, sales staff and service repair technicians are the agents who "bear" knowledge, and cross professional and licensing boundaries to share information with other professionals about how things work.

The individuals in the firms communicate with individuals in other firms at continuing education and professional trade meetings.

It is a distinct form of knowledge called "tacit" knowledge.

Tacit knowledge is the knowledge that humans, carry around in their heads. Tacit knowledge, in its economic context, is created, and is diffused among a distinct economic population, primarily the scientific, technical and engineering staff of manufacturing firms.

These agents consume knowledge, and their pursuit of knowledge becomes an important activity in understanding the evolution of technology.

Tacit knowledge, in the theory of technology evolution, builds upon what exists in the memories of humans, and knowledge is cumulative, in the sense that it builds upon existing memories.

The social/business networks that exist within the economy serve as the institutional framework for knowledge creation and diffusion.

New technological knowledge is diffused within the social networks when the scientific and technical staff meet each other, in face-to-face encounters. The reason that face-to-face engagements are so important to the theory of technology evolution relates to how humans interpret each other's behavior.

The other form of knowledge, not dependent on social network interaction, is "codified" knowledge, which is contained in written documents and technical manuals.

The codified knowledge is easier for corporate elites to control than tacit knowledge, and is easier for the Chinese to steal, because the global corporate elites can control who has access to the codified knowledge.

The exclusive reliance on codified knowledge, inside the global corporate firm, acts to limit the application of new technology, even if a boundary-spanner, or some other scientific staff, happened to bring knowledge into the firm.

The creation of new technological knowledge precedes the diffusion of knowledge through the social business networks. Both types of processes rely on the existence of business/social networks.

According to George Korres, et al., diffusion is the last step in the chronology of the impact technological innovation on economic development. Korres writes,

"Schumpeter states that the major long-term fluctuations in economic development cannot be explained by terms of conventional short and medium term business cycle theory but require an additional dimension of analysis. This involves the rise of new technologies, the rise and decline of entire industries, major infrastructural investments, changes in the international location of industry and technological leadership and other related structural changes, for instance, in the skills and composition of labour force and the management structure of enterprises…the rate of diffusion determines to a large extent the rate of technological change measured as the effect of an innovation on productivity increase in an industry. On the other hand, diffusion plays an important part in the competitive process in the sense that diffusion deteriorates the competitive edge which is maintained by

the originator of successful innovations. Schumpeter had classified technological change in the following, steps:
(a) the invention;
(b) the innovation and
(c) the diffusion.

Diffusion is the last step jn the economic impact of a new product or process." (Korres, George, M., Lionaki, Irene, and Polichronopoulos, George, The Role of Technical Change and Diffusion In Schumpeterian Lines, in Backhaus, J., (ed.), Joseph Alois Schumpeter, Kluwer Academic Publishers, 2003.).

Peter J. Boettke et al., describes tacit knowledge as an economic asset that can be increased, under the right set of constitutional rules and social institutions.

In other words, placing Schumpeter's knowledge creation and diffusion form of entrepreneurial capitalism into Buchanan's constitutional framework would create an inexhaustible economic growth asset for a society, which then leads to the emergence of a stable social order.

Boettke writes,

"The stock of local and tacit knowledge of "how to get things done" within the polycentric system can be seen as a spontaneous order that is continually changing. What can be called the cultural aspects of the social order, how to interact with others, solve problems, and so on can be characterized as a spontaneous order. Individuals purposefully interact with others, but the set of norms that evolve are an unintended result of those purposeful interactions…We need an institutional environment [Buchanan's institutions] that is malleable and can handle ever-changing circumstances. In sum, the very notion of spontaneous order [that emerges from economic exchange] expunges any notion of a static equilibrium and requires an emphasis on the mechanisms that allow individuals to deal with unique situations that arise." (Boettke, Peter J., and , Coyne, Christopher, Methodological Individualism, Spontaneous Order and the Research Program of the Workshop in Political Theory and Policy Analysis, George Mason University, Department of Economics, 2004.).

We place Schumpeter's entrepreneurial capitalist theory into Buchanan's characterization of the productive and protective state to derive economic principles for a new constitution.

The synthesis of thought leads to a state sovereignty, decentralized national structure of government, based upon

Mason's principle that all legitimate government power is derived from the consent of the governed.

In Buchanan's constitutional rules, the government power can be characterized as the "productive" state, whose power is directed to protecting the rules of free market exchange in economic transactions.

The power of government, for Buchanan, can also be characterized as the "protective" state, whose power is directed to protecting the individual natural and civil rights of citizens, in political exchanges among citizens, and between a citizen and the agencies of government.

All power of government flows from the Preamble of Mason's Virginia Declaration of Rights, which states that the mission of government is to protect the rights of individual citizens, in contrast to Madison's Preamble which seeks to balance power among two social classes.

Mason placed his entire Declaration of Rights at the beginning of his Virginia Constitution of 1776, and we excerpt the most important elements here, and agree with Mason that the entire set of principles should be placed at the beginning of the new national constitution.

Section 1. That all men are by nature equally free and independent and have certain inherent rights, of which, when they enter into a state of society, they cannot, by any compact, deprive or divest their posterity; namely, the enjoyment of life and liberty, with the means of acquiring and possessing property, and pursuing and obtaining happiness and safety.

Section 2. That all power is vested in, and consequently derived from, the people; that magistrates are their trustees and servants and at all times amenable to them.

Section 3. That government is, or ought to be, instituted for the common benefit, protection, and security of the people, nation, or community; of all the various modes and forms of government, that is best which is capable of producing the greatest degree of happiness and safety and is most effectually secured against the danger of maladministration. And that, when any government shall be found inadequate or contrary to these purposes, a majority of the community has an indubitable, inalienable, and indefeasible right to reform, alter, or abolish it, in such manner as shall be judged most conducive to the public weal.

Section 4. That elections of members to serve as representatives of the people, in assembly ought to be free; and that all men, having sufficient evidence of permanent common interest with, and attachment to, the community, have the right of suffrage and cannot be taxed or deprived of their property for public uses without their own consent or that of their representatives so elected, nor bound by any law to which they have not, in like manner, assented, for the public good.

In terms of economic exchange, Mason highlights the right of citizens to acquire and use property, which is linked to Buchanan's principles of the productive state.

Mason states that citizens have the right of,

"The means of acquiring and possessing property, and pursuing and obtaining happiness and safety."

An essential distinction between Mason's principles and Madison's constitution is that rights inure to individual citizens, not to social classes or synthetic legal entities, like corporations.

As Madison's collectivist principles evolved, in the mid-1880s, natural human rights were extended to corporations, as if corporations were just like individual humans.

That evolutionary treatment of corporations and banks has resulted in the unelected power of corporations to coerce and repress individual citizens, using the undelegated power of government agencies, abetted by the power of the Fed to manipulate money supply.

Buchanan adds the constitutional principles of the productive state:

The constitutional purpose of the productive state is to protect and promote national economic sovereignty from foreign and domestic enemies.

The productive state seeks to promote national economic growth with maximum distribution of benefits to all social classes so that all citizens benefit from economic growth.

The productive state manages the money supply as a medium of exchange whose future standard of value is linked to the growth of national GDP.

The productive state eliminates the discretionary power of the Fed to manipulate the supply of money, the creation of debt, and interest rates, in favor of market based interest rates established in currency exchange markets, and commodity future exchanges.

The constitution of the productive state demands that the government operate on a national annual balanced budget, with current tax rates not to exceed the expected tax revenues, in any two year budget cycle.

The constitution of the productive state establishes written constitutional rules that future increases in tax rates are linked to the increase in the rate of economic growth in the national GDP, with specific identification of the sources of future tax revenues, linked to the national annual budget.

The productive state demands that the annual increase in national debt be approved by the legislatures of 2/3s of the states.

The productive state national constitution authorizes and charters a decentralized state and regional banking institutional framework, similar in concept to the free banking era between 1840 and 1913.

Of all of Buchanan's constitutional principles for applying Schumpeter's entrepreneurial economy, the most important is a stable money supply and predictable money values.

A stable, predictable national monetary policy provides a context of financial stability for the entrepreneur as he makes his guesses about the future demand for his products.

If the supply of money is stable and the future value predictable, the economic conditions are favorable for capital investment which promotes continued technical change and innovation.

A productive national government would promote the deferment of capital gains tax on reinvestment of profits from entrepreneurial exit events.

Buchanan's protective state aims at the creation of equal individual opportunity to achieve happiness and prosperity through individual initiative. All of Mason's principles of government in his Virginia Declaration of Rights would be protected by the protective state.

The entire edifice of Buchanan's constitution rests upon the equal application of the law to all citizens. The equal opportunity for financial success is the glue that binds citizens to obey the rule of law.

Buchanan's principles of political exchange allows for the emergence of a stable social order of voluntary allegiance of citizens to obey the rule of law

Only free market and free political exchange, in Buchanan's framework, allows citizens the individual liberty to discover future market value, and only entrepreneurial capitalism can overcome the unequal initial distribution of wealth between social classes at the beginning of any evolutionary period.

The principles of the constitution of the protective state include rules on:

- Rules on economic competition and prohibitions on monopoly or unfair and deceptive trade practices.
- Rules on fair access to loans and capital to start new ventures or expand existing business.
- Protection of open flows of information and knowledge for technology innovation.
- Protection of national sovereign technology innovation and intellectual property rights.
- Rules on the prohibition on special interest corporate lobbying and rule manipulation and conflict of interest of government agents and elected representatives to use the agencies of government to limit competition or direct the benefits of economic growth to their own social class.

We conclude that the progress towards a fair American entrepreneurial constitution can be improved by visualizing Buchanan's constitutional rules and Schumpeter's entrepreneurial economy as a knowledge creation enterprise, whose end goal is the commercialization of radical new technology, and the creation of new future markets.

It was this ability of Jefferson's small yeoman farmers, and the ensuing development of American small businesses, in each metro region, that created the American middle class.

The American middle and working classes emerged as a consequence of national economic growth.

The economic growth in America was caused by entrepreneurial technology innovation and the technology commercialization in small entrepreneurial firms.

The American economy and economic growth was permanently damaged when the global crony corporations moved the intermediate demand chains to China, beginning in 1992.

The damage caused to American technology innovation by exporting the intermediate demand chains occurred in the "knowledge creation-knowledge diffusion linkages in the supply chains among small manufacturing firms. (Vass, Laurie Thomas, Theory of Technology Evolution, Gabby Press, 2019.).

The synthesis of thought of Mason/Buchanan/Schumpeter offers a logical, coherent theory of constitutional rules and economic theory to re-create Schumpeter's decentralized entrepreneurial capitalist economy in the sovereign states of America.

Chapter 7. George Mason's America: The Emergence of A Stable State Sovereignty Entrepreneurial Capitalist Society.

Our intent in this book has been to argue that Mason's egalitarian concept of political rights, had it been implemented in 1787, would have been a better path for liberty for American middle and working class citizens, than Madison's framework, that ended with the agencies of government in the hands of an unelected deep state ruling class tyranny.

The thesis of the book is that a new constitution with Mason's concept of individual liberty, placed within Buchanan's constitutional framework, and Schumpeter's entrepreneurial capitalist economy provides a pathway for American citizens back to the original intent of George Mason and Thomas Jefferson, in their respective documents of 1776.

The synthesis of thought of Mason, Buchanan, and Schumpeter provides the starting point of the national debate over what form of government replaces Madison's flawed constitution.

Our premise in arguing for a new constitution to replace Madison's constitution is that his representative republic ended in November of 2020, with massive election fraud.

His centralized government became disconnected from the consent of the governed, and the central government adopted a will of its own, independent of the will of the citizens.

There is nothing in Madison's rules that prevents the government, or the agents of the deep state, from abusing the power of government to pursue their own interests at the expense of common citizens.

We agree with Noah Feldman that Madison's constitution is too broken to be repaired, through amendments. (Feldman, Noah, The Broken Constitution: Lincoln, Slavery, and the Refounding of America, Farrar, Straus & Giroux, 2021.)

The primary defect in Madison's constitution originates in his conception of the supreme sovereignty of the central government as a protector of rights. Citizens cannot trust agents of government to protect their rights, or for the agents of government to abide by the rule of law.

The politically-correct view that government can be safely trusted to operate in the public interest is false.

One of Buchanan's points about political exchange is that citizens must expect that the agents of government are engaged in operating the government against the long-term public interest, in favor of serving the short-term financial advantages of the ruling class.

Madison's conception of the supreme sovereignty of the central government is based upon a false premise.

Bernard Bailyn, in The Ideological Origins of the American Revolution, explains the false premise and asks what happens if Madison's conception of government sovereignty turns out to be a consolidated central tyranny?

Bailyn asks:

"What if the sense of the constitution (as protector of rights) proved false and it came to be believed that the force of government threatened rather than protected these rights?"

As both Mason and Jefferson wrote, in 1776, what happens next, when the government becomes destructive of the ends for which it is created, is that citizens have the God-given right to alter or abolish the government.

We argue for abolishing Madison's constitution, and starting over with a new constitution in a decentralized, state sovereignty, entrepreneurial capitalist nation.

The first step in starting over is for each state legislature to appoint a Commission for the analysis of the defects in Madison's rules, and to use the Commission's final report as the basis for the citizens of each state to vote to adopt a new national constitution.

Mason's new constitutional framework that begins with the Preamble of state sovereignty, based upon individual freedom, as the purpose of the national constitution, would allow the citizens of each state to choose between the status quo of Madison's broken constitution, and a superior form of a decentralized representative democracy.

The constitutional public purpose in the new nation is served when government acts to create the institutional and social framework for individual citizens to pursue their self destiny.

Within that context of individual freedom, the free market serves as the mechanism through which individuals derive their incomes and future wealth.

The role of government is to protect citizen liberty and provide fair rules of open competition and a secure, stable legal environment for market exchange transactions.

We offer Mason's 12 modified and updated constitutional provisions which establish the state sovereignty framework of individual economic and political freedom:

1. The National Congress shall have the power to issue government bonds, and to borrow money on the credit of the Democratic Republic of America. All proposals to borrow money or issue debt shall occur

once in the two year budget cycle, and all proposals to issue debt must be approved by 50% of the State legislatures of the Democratic Republic of America, no later than January 21 of the year of issuance.
2. The term of debt and interest on any issuance of debt shall not exceed 10 years, and must be paid in full by the end of the 10th year.
3. The aggregate debt of the nation, in any five year period, shall not exceed 20% of the average GDP of that five year period, the GDP to be recalculated at the end of every five year period.
4. The National Congress shall have the power to regulate commerce and approve trade agreements with foreign nations, which are negotiated by the President, and ratified by a majority vote of both houses of Congress.
5. The National Congress shall have the power to establish a uniform rule of citizen naturalization, and provide revenues for national border security to prohibit illegal entrance into the sovereign nation or any sovereign state.
6. The National Congress shall have the power to coin money, regulate the value thereof, regulate the circulation and creation of money and money instruments, regulate the national banking system and establish the currency value of foreign coin, and fix the Standard of Weights and Measures.
7. The National Congress shall have the power to provide for the punishment for the national criminal

felony of counterfeiting the securities and money of the Democratic Republic of America.
8. The National Congress shall have the power to establish a national Post Office and a national system of roads and transportation routes, and national regulation of any form of internet communication that limits free speech.
9. The National Congress shall have the power to authorize regional capital securities markets, and to establish regulatory guidelines for the operation of regional private and public security exchanges designed to promote maximum national and regional economic growth rates.
10. The National Congress shall have the power to establish and maintain a
 national patent office to promote the progress of science and useful arts, by securing for limited times to authors and inventors the exclusive right to their respective writings and discoveries.
11. The National Congress shall have the power to protect the patents of citizens from foreign and domestic criminal usurpation of the right of citizens to enjoy the benefits of their invention.
12. The National Congress shall have the power to define and punish intellectual property piracies and criminal patent felonies committed against citizens of the Democratic Republic of America by foreign and domestic criminals.

The unchecked power of government to borrow and issue bonds, in principles 1 2, 3, above, must be limited by constitutional prohibitions. Except in the extreme emergency of a declaration of war, by the majority of both houses of Congress, the aggregate national debt cannot exceed 20% of the national GDP.

Buchanan explained that borrowing today for future consumption rather than current period investment, permanently retards the rate of economic growth, and rewards the asset speculation of the ruling class.

The burden of government debt is borne by common citizens in the future, not the investment bankers and asset speculators who benefit from the government borrowing, in the current time period.

Central government budget deficits make it possible for the agents of government to spend tax dollars, today, without taxing. Whether the deficit is created through reduced taxes or increased expenditures, the form of borrowing will determine the distribution of gains among social classes.

The discretionary power of the Fed to set monetary policy and issue debt must be taken away from them, or any other future central bank.

The rate of monetary growth must be established by constitutional rules.

The monetary base of the total money supply should be established by rule that the growth rate of money is equal to the annual rate of the economic growth of national GDP.

In the event of an economic depression that results in zero growth of the GDP, the rate of money growth is linked to the rate established in the previous year of the growth of the GDP.

The standard of value of the money created by the central government is not linked to some commodity, such as gold, or silver. The standard of value is the economic growth rate of the national GDP, which inspires confidence of financial institutions and citizens in the value of money as seen as a unit of exchange, not a store of value.

Buchanan suggests that the goal of monetary policy is future predictability of the rate of money creation, and stability in the value of money. The policy of predictability and stability would allow all entrepreneurs and investors to share confidence in the stability of the new national economy.

Buchanan's foundational premise of creating a new constitution is that it be based upon the individual, not social groups. The newly-created constitution must be ratified by individual citizens to establish the legitimate authority of the constitution.

In the logic of Buchanan's public choice theory, his principles would be called methodological individualism.

In leaving the imaginary state of nature, and agreeing to be governed by a constitution, the individual exchanges his own liberty with others who similarly give up liberties in exchange for the benefits offered to all citizens by a constitution characterized by natural rights protection for all, and special privileges for none.

In giving up individual natural rights, the individual citizen seeks to protect their natural rights, not given up, as written and codified in the constitution that they create.

These written rights are commonly called a Bill of Rights, which is the first part of Mason's constitution, which he called the Virginia Declaration of Rights.

We offer a synthesis of Mason's original individual rights, of 1776, supplemented by Buchanan's theory of methodological individualism.

Citizen Bill of Rights of the Democratic Republic of America.

In creating this constitution, we affirm and swear that all citizens in each of the respective States are guaranteed equal rights for all, and special privileges for none.

Among these rights are:

1. That all citizens have a natural right to worship and exercise their own religion and that the National Government is prohibited from making and enforcing any law respecting the establishment of an official national religion and compelling citizens to worship a national religion.
2. The National Government shall be prohibited from making or enforcing any law that restricts the natural right of a citizen's freedom of speech and freedom of conscience.
3. The National Government is prohibited from making or enforcing any law which restricts the right of citizens to peaceably assemble, and to petition the National Government for a redress of grievances.
4. That all citizens have a natural right to truthful and honest statements from government agents and from elected representatives, and that it is the duty of the free press to report the truth.
5. That all citizens in the respective states have a natural right to own and use weapons, and that the

National Government, nor any state, shall make no laws which abridge the right of law-abiding citizens from owning, keeping and bearing weapons.
6. The National Government is prohibited from using agents of government or national resources to conduct searches and seizures of private citizen documents, or property, and that the possessions and documents obtained from illegal searches and seizures are inadmissible in any national court.
7. No citizen in any state shall be seized or imprisoned, or stripped of his rights or of his property or possessions, or outlawed or exiled, or deprived of his standing in any other way, nor shall agents of the government proceed with force against him, or send others to do so, except by the lawful judgment of a true bill of indictment by a majority vote of a grand jury of 18 citizens, or by the rules of judicial civil procedure of the National Government.
8. No warrants or judicial orders in any criminal investigation shall be issued by a national court, except upon probable cause, determined in a judicial hearing, supported by an oath or affirmation of the government agent describing the specific items or locations to be searched and a judicial description of the crime being investigated.

9. No person shall be held to answer for a capital, or otherwise infamous crime, unless on a presentment or indictment of a majority vote of a Grand Jury of 18 citizens who conduct an inquiry into the legitimacy of the government's allegation of a national crime.
10. No citizen shall be subject for the same offence or to be twice put in jeopardy of life or limb; nor shall be compelled in any criminal case to be a witness against himself.
11. The National Government, and every State government, are prohibited from making or enforcing any law which shall abridge the privileges or immunities of citizens of the States; nor shall any State deprive any natural human person of life, liberty, or property, without due process of law; nor deny to any person within its jurisdiction the equal protection of the laws.
12. No citizen shall be deprived of life, liberty, or property, without due process of law; nor shall private property be taken for public use, without just compensation, determined by a majority vote of a Grand Jury of 18 citizens.
13. That all citizens are due the equal application of justice and that no citizen, elected representative, or

agent of government, is entitled to special or unequal treatment of the application of the law.

14. That all citizens in any criminal or civil proceeding, are presumed innocent until proven guilty in a trial of due process, by a jury of 12 of their peers.

15. In all criminal prosecutions, the accused shall enjoy the right to a speedy and public trial, within 6 months of indictment, by an impartial jury of the State and district wherein the crime shall have been committed, which district shall have been previously ascertained by law, and to be informed of the nature and cause of the accusation; to be confronted with the witnesses against him; to have compulsory process for obtaining witnesses in his favor, and to have the assistance of counsel for his defense.

16. The right of trial by jury shall be preserved, and no fact tried by a jury, shall be otherwise re-examined in any Court of the States, than according to the rules of the common law then obtaining in the national judiciary.

17. Excessive bail shall not be required, nor excessive fines imposed, nor cruel and unusual punishments inflicted, nor imprisonment for longer than 5 days, in the absence of specific charges and allegation of crime.

18. That citizens have a civil right of action against elected representatives or agents of the National Government, for violation of these natural rights, upon a presentation of a motion of grievance to a Grand Jury of 18 citizens, who shall hear the case and determine the outcome and set the penalties for the violation by a majority vote.
19. The a citizens Grand Jury in any State retains the right of initiating a citizen initiative on legislative proposals or access to government documents, by a petition to the House of Representatives, which must respond to the petition within 30 days of receipt.
20. The right of citizens of the States to vote, hold elected office, or deliberate in public debates, shall not be denied or abridged by the National Government or by any State on account of race, color of skin, biological sex, or religious beliefs.
21. The right of a citizen to vote in all elections is an inviolable inalienable natural right, and is constitutionally protected, in both the citizen's freedom to vote and in the legitimate count of the vote, in all local, state, and national elections and referendums, by Federal and State law enforcement agents.

The Preamble of the new constitution states the mission and purpose of the new government.

As we noted above, in Chapter 3, Madison's preamble is a nominal nothing because his phrase "to form a more perfect union," could mean anything.

We offer a synthesis of Mason's original constitution of Virginia, with Buchanan's methodological individualism to establish the mission of the new government.

The Preamble states:

We, the citizens of the states of Democratic Republic of America, establish this constitutional contract between our respective states and the National Government of the Democratic Republic of America.

"We solemnly swear and affirm that we establish this contract to preserve and protect the natural and civil rights of citizens in each state, and to protect and defend the sovereignty of each state and the nation, from foreign and domestic threats."

Guiding Principles of the Democratic Republic of America National Government.

By freely and voluntarily joining our state government into the union of the Democratic Republic of America, we affirm that the National Government will be guided by the following principles:

1. "...that all legitimate government authority is derived from the consent of the citizens governed..."
2. "...that as the consequence of the sovereign authority of citizens, citizens have an inalienable natural right to remove, within 30 days, an elected representative from office upon a referendum of 51% of registered voters in a state..."
3. "...that those governed by the laws and whose individual freedom is restricted by the laws should have the greatest say and consent in making of the laws..."
4. "...that those who make the laws and give consent to the laws, acting as representatives of the citizens, bind themselves and their constituents to following the laws..."
5. "...that the National Government is instituted to allow individual citizens to pursue individual happiness and to limit the arbitrary application of government power over the lives of individuals..."
6. "...that individual citizens who freely give their consent to form a government through constitutional conventions are bound by the original contract until the operation of the government becomes destructive

to the original intent of obtaining individual freedom and the pursuit of happiness..."
7. "...that the citizens of each state have mechanisms in place in the constitutional contract to modify or abolish the governments that have been created that have become destructive to the ideals and goals under which the National Government is instituted, including the right to vote on remaining a member of the national government in a referendum to be held every 20 years from the date of admittance..."
8. "...that the parties to the constitutional contract are individual human citizens acting through their elected representatives at the state and national levels of government..."
9. "...that the National Government is created by this union of states and the National Government has no independent powers except for those expressly delegated to it by the states, and that the national government shall never usurp the sovereign power or authority of the individual states or the sovereignty of the citizens in each state and that states have an inalienable right to call a convention of the states, without Congressional approval, to modify, amend, or abolish this Constitutional Contract."
10. "...that an individual's private property obtained through legal contract and title transfer, their rights to appropriate income and profits from the use of their private property, and their rights to dispose and

transfer their private property are inviolate and derived from natural rights granted to them by God, and that no government or constitutional contract may ever abrogate or subordinate these natural individual rights, unless by free and voluntary consent of the citizen..."

11. "...that a citizens Grand Jury of 18 citizens is impaneled, for a term of 12 months, to protect and preserve the rights of citizens against the arbitrary application of government power against citizens..."

12. "...that a citizens Grand Jury of 18 citizens must inspect all national penal facilities within its district every 6 months, and report their findings to the Chief District Judge, who shall act to remedy the deficiencies found by the Grand Jury..."

13. "...that the 1776 Declaration of Independence established a representative democracy, ordained by God, to pursue individual human freedoms and liberty from oppression and is an exceptional model in human history to be preserved, protected, and cherished by the citizens and deployed by them and their elected representatives as the guiding principles in the Democratic Republic of America in its relationships with other nations and other people..."

In her book, George Mason: Constitutionalist, Helen Hill describes the debate during the 1787 convention in terms of sectionalism, meaning that the northern states did not want to form a centralized union with the southern slaveocracy.

During the convention, the delegates made many references to not forming a union, or that if a union was formed, under the sectionalist conflict that the union would end in a civil war.

Hill writes,

"The sense of sectionalism became so strong that some of the members saw no solution but to organize two confederacies…on July 13 Morris stated, "Instead of attempting to blend incompatible things, let us at once take friendly leave of each other."…on July 23 Pinckney "reminded the Convention that if the Constitution should fail to insert some security to the Southern States against an emancipation of slaves and taxes on exports, he should be bound by duty to his State to vote against their report," (Peter Smith Edition, 1966.).

The historical debate over leaving the Union and forming a new separate nation, in alliance with Great Britain, was renewed by the New England states, during the War of 1812, at their Harford Convention.

Prior to the start of the Civil War, General Winfred Scott advised Lincoln to "Let our Southern sisters go in peace."

We argue that Madison's effort to combine two distinct cultures, under one centralized government was a failure.

In 1787, the northern states did not share common cultural values with the southern slaveocracy, and forcing the two alien cultures to combine, under his constitution did not result in peace or freedom.

Madison's 235 year legacy is not characterized as social peace and harmony among social classes or among the races.

The Madison and Hamilton financial system did not result in economic stability or national economic growth that benefitted all social classes.

Likewise, today two alien cultures do not co-exist in peace, and do not share common cultural or philosophical principles on the mission of the national government.

We argue that the differences are irreconcilable, and cannot be remedied by amendments or modifications to Madison's document.

We agree with the analysis of Madison's rules by Richard Henry Lee, who wrote,

"So extensive a territory as that of the U. States. . . cannot be governed in freedom, unless formed into States sovereign and confederated for Common good....In the latter case, {confederated state sovereignty] opinion, founded in the knowledge of those who govern, Procures obedience without force. But remove opinion, which must fall with a knowledge of characters in so widely extended a country, and force then becomes necessary to secure the purposes of Civil society. All governments depend on support and assistance from their citizens, for which there are two sources: free assent or forced compliance." (Ballagh, James Curtis, The Letters of Richard Henry Lee, The MacMillan Company, 2014.).

Herbert J. Storing, in his exhaustive work on the anti-federalist arguments against ratification of Madison's documents writes,

"The disagreement between supporters and opponents of the Constitution was an argument about the viability of a republican government of unprecedented scale and scope. The Anti-Federalist understanding of attachment [of citizens to the new nation] was a central component of their support for government that was small, simple, and close to the people A corollary of these commitments was that the people must exert significant control over their representatives, in the form of elections at short intervals, brief tenure in office, and districts of limited size. Each of these structural implications would make the workings of government discernible to all, thus encouraging citizens to render 'their freely given support." (Storing, Herbert, ed., George Mason and George Washington: What the Anti-Federalists Were For, University of Chicago Press, 1981.).

Madison's rules were a failure because his rules did not offer a common set of moral values that bound citizen voluntary allegiance to obey the rule of law. And, as Richard Henry Lee points out, in the absence of voluntary citizen allegiance, there is only the coercive police power of the state to enforce obedience to the rule of law. [Leviathan].

Madison's rules were also a failure because he ignored the principles of Montesquieu about the virtues of a small republic. The only way Madiosn's flawed defective extended republic could have worked is in a decentralized, state sovereignty framework.

In making his application of the economic exchange model to political exchange, Buchanan emphasized the ability of citizens to opt out of economic contracts.

Buchanan referred to this property of economic exchange as the freedom to escape from coercive or repressive economic conditions, for example, slavery.

When he applied this concept of escape from repression to the political exchange model, Buchanan noted that he agreed with Mason and Jefferson that citizens have a natural right to alter or abolish the government, as a way of escape.

Buchanan wrote,

"The exit option for states…the separate states, individually or in groups must be constitutionally empowered to secede from the federalized political structure to form new units of political authority beyond the reach of the existing federal government…otherwise the federal government may extract surplus value from the citizens almost at will, because there is no effective means of escape." (Buchanan, James M., The Collected Works of James M Buchanan, Vol. 18. Federalism, Liberty, and the Law. The Liberty Fund, 2001.).

The anti-federalists were well aware of Madison's defects of his consolidated central government, and fought valiantly for state sovereignty, in a grossly unfair and fraudulent ratification scheme.

Jacob T. Levy explains, in Beyond Publius, the logic of the anti-federalist argument by citing both Publius and Jefferson,

Levy writes,

"Publius' argument [for state sovereignty] depends upon the greater affection or sympathy the people naturally feel for the states than for the federal government. Long after the Kentucky and Virginia Resolutions, Jefferson continued to warn of the dangers of consolidated government, warning that federalism [state sovereignty] as intellectually akin to the separation of powers. "When all government, domestic and foreign, in little, as in great things, shall be drawn to Washington as the center of all power, it will render powerless the checks and balances provided one government on another, and will become as venal and oppressive as the government from which we separated. [Great Britian] Jefferson stated that a "large republic could better protect freedom than a small one, but only if, and in part, because of it was organized with both separation of powers and federalism [state sovereignty]."

(Levy, Jacob T., Beyond Publius: Montesquieu, Liberal Republicanism and the Small-Republic Thesis, JSTOR, 2006.).

Publius, Mason, Jefferson, and Buchanan were correct about the inherent dangers of Madison's rules, and citizens are now confronted with correcting the centralized ruling class tyranny, that never should have been allowed to metastasize.

We argue that there is only one pathway back to freedom, and taking that path means starting over, with a new constitution, at the point in history when Mason and Jefferson wrote their respective documents, in 1776.

Bibliography

Aligica, Paul, et al., Exploring The Political Economy and Social Philosophy of James M. Buchanan, Rowman & Littlefield, 2018.

Bailyn, Bernard, The Ideological Origins of the American Revolution, Belknap Press, 2017.

Ballagh, James Curtis, The Letters of Richard Henry Lee, The MacMillan Company, 2014.

Balogh, Brian, A Government Out of Sight: The Mystery of National Authority in Nineteenth-Century America, Cambridge University Press, 2009.

Beard, Charles A., An Economic Interpretation of the Constitution of the United States. The Macmillan Company. 1914.

Bernstein, Richard, The Founding Fathers Reconsidered, Oxford University Press, 2011.

Boettke, Peter J.. et al., Money as Meta-Rule: Buchanan's Constitutional Economics as a Foundation for Monetary Stability, AIER Sound Money Project Working Paper No. 2018–12, 2018.

Boettke, Peter J. and Coyne, Christopher J., Methodological Individualism, Spontaneous Order and the Research Program of the Workshop in Political Theory and Policy Analysis, George Mason University, Department of Economics, 2004.

Branson, Margaret Stimmann, George Mason: The Reluctant Founder, Internet blog, Center for Civic Education. ND.

Brennan, Geoffrey and Buchanan, James M., The Reason of Rules: Constitutional Political Economy, Cambridge University Press, 2008.

Broadwater, Jeff, George Mason: The Forgotten Founder.UNC Press, 2006.

Buchanan, James M., Constitutional Economics, Blackwell Publishing, 1991.

Buchanan, James M., Economic Freedom and Federalism: Prospect for a New Century, The Collected Works of James Buchanan, The Liberty Fund, 2001

Buchanan, James M., The Collected Works of James M Buchanan, Vol. 18. Federalism, Liberty, and the Law. The Liberty Fund, 2001.

Buchanan, James, M., The Limits of Liberty: Between Anarchy and Leviathan, University of Chicago Press, 1975.

Buchanan, James M., The Logical Foundations of Constitutional Liberty, Liberty Fund, 1999.

Buchanan, James M., and Tullock, Gordon, The Calculus of Consent: Logical Foundations of Constitutional Democracy (The Collected Works of) Liberty Fund; Volume 3 ed., 1999.

Codevilla, Angelo The Ruling Class: How They Corrupted America and What We Can Do About It, Beaufort Books, 2010.

Congleton, Roger D., The Contractarian Constitutional Political Economy of James Buchanan, West Virginia University Press, 2013.

Copeland, Pamela and MacMaster, Richard, The Five George Masons: Patriots and Planters of Virginia and Maryland, University of Virginia Press, 1975.

Cornell, Saul, The Other Founders, UNC Press, 1999.

Domhoff, William, Who Rules America? Power and Politics in the Year 2006, Routledge, 8th edition, 2021.

Driesbach, Daniel, George Mason's Pursuit of Religious Liberty in Revolutionary Virginia, Gunston Gazette, Vol. 2, No. 2, 1997.

Evangelista, Rinaldo, Knowledge and Investment: The Sources of Innovation in Industry, Edward Elgar Publishing, 1999.

Farber, Daniel A., The Fourteenth Amendment and the Unconstitutionality of Secession, Akron Law Review, 2015.

Farrand, Max, ed.. The Records of the Federal Convention of 1787. 4 vols. Yale University Press. 1966.

Feldman, Noah, The Broken Constitution: Lincoln, Slavery, and the Refounding of America, Farrar, Straus & Giroux, 2021.

Florida, Richard, The Distinct Personality of Entrepreneurial Cities, Bloomberg News, 2015.

Foner, Philip S., ed., The Complete Writings of Thomas Paine in Two Volumes, The Citadel Press, 1945.

Gallatin, Albert, A Sketch of the Finances of the United States, W.A. Davis, 1796.

Goodwyn, Lawrence, The Populist Moment: A Short History of the Agrarian Revolt in America, Oxford University Press, 1978.

Henriques, Peter, An Uneven Friendship, The Virginia Magazine of History and Biography, 1989.

Hill, Helen, George Mason: Constitutionalist, Peter Smith Edition, 1966.

Hilferding, Rudolf, Finance Capital. A Study of the Latest Phase of Capitalist Development. Bottomore, Tom, ed., Routledge, 1981.

Hobbes, Thomas, Leviathan, 1651, reprinted by Clarendon Press, 1909.

Hoffert, Robert, A Politics of Tensions: The Articles of Confederation and American Political Ideas, University Press of Colorado, 1992.

Hyland, William G., George Mason: The Founding Father Who Gave Us The Bill of Rights, Regnery History, 2019.

Jackson, Jonathan. Thoughts Upon the Political Situation of the United States of America: In which that of

Massachusetts is More Particularly Considered. With Some Observations on the Constitution for a Federal Government. Addressed to the People of the Union, 1788.

Jefferson, Thomas, Opinion on the Constitutionality of the Bill for Establishing a National Bank, 1791.

Jensen, Merrill, The Articles of Confederation, University of Wisconsin Press, 1970.

Kaminsky, John and Leffler, Richard, Federalists and Antifederalists: The Debate Over the Ratification of the Constitution, Madison House, 1998.

Kindleberger, Charles P., World Economic Primacy: 1500-1990, Oxford University Press, 1996.

Klarman, Michael, The Framers Coup, Oxford University Press, 2016.

Korres, George M., Lionaki, Irene, and Polichronopoulos, George, The Role of Technical Change and Diffusion In Schumpeterian Lines, in Backhaus, J., (ed.), Joseph Alois Schumpeter, Kluwer Academic Publishers, 2003.

Kukla, Jon, Yes! No! and If!, internet blog article, ND.

Levine, Rhonda, Social Class and Stratification: Classic Statements and Theoretical Debates, Rowman & Littlefield, 2006.

Levy, Jacob T., Beyond Publius: Montesquieu, Liberal Republicanism and the Small-Republic Thesis, JSTOR, 2006.

March, Raymond J., The Substance of Entrepreneurship and the Entrepreneurship of Substances, et al., SSRN, 2016.

Mason, Robert C., George Mason of Virginia, Oscar Aurlius Morgner, 1919.

McDonald. Forrest, A Constitutional History of the United States. Franklin Watts, 1982.

Miller, Helen Hill, George Mason: Gentleman Revolutionary, UNC Press, 1975.

Mokyr, Joel, The Gifts of Athena: Historical Origins of the Knowledge Economy, Princeton University Press, 2002.

Mokyr, Joel, The Lever of Riches: Technological Creativity and Economic Progress, Oxford University Press, 1990.

Morton, Joseph C., The Constitutional Convention of 1787: A Biographical Dictionary, Greenwood Press, 2006.

Pacheco, Josephine, Antifederalism: The Legacy of George Mason, George Mason University Press, 1992.

Pacheco, Josephine, The Legacy of George Mason, George Mason University Press, 1983.

Rakove, Jack, Original Meanings: Politics and Ideas in the Making of the Constitution A.A. Knopf, 1996.

Rutland, Robert, George Mason: Reluctant Statesman LSU Press. Kindle Edition. 1961.

Schumpeter, Joseph A., Business Cycles: A Theoretical, Historical, and Statistical Analysis of the Capitalist Process, McGraw-Hill Book Company. 1939.

Schumpeter, Joseph, A., Capitalism, Socialism, and Democracy, Harper Perennial, 1962.

Buchanan, James A., Economic Freedom and Federalism: Prospect for a New Century, The Collected Works of James Buchanan, The Liberty Fund, 2001.

Schumpeter, Joseph A., Essays On Entrepreneurs, Innovations, Business Cycles and the Evolution of Capitalism, Clemence, Richard V., ed., Routledge, 1989.

Schumpeter, Joseph A., History of Economic Analysis. Oxford University Press, 1954.

Schumpeter, Joseph A. The Economics of Sociology and Capitalism, Nee, Victor, and Swedberg, Richard, eds. Princeton University Press. 1991.

Schumpeter, Joseph A. The Explanation of the Business Cycle, Reprinted in Joseph A. Schumpeter, Essays on Entrepreneurs, Innovations, Business Cycles, and the Evolution of Capitalism, Transaction, 1927.

Schumpeter, Joseph A., The Theory of Economic Development, Harvard University Press, 1934.

Schumpeter, Joseph A. The Sociology of Imperialisms, in Schumpeter, Joseph A., Imperialism and Social Classes, Sweezy, Paul M.,ed., Blackwell, 1951.

Senese, Donald, George Mason and the Legacy of Constitutional Liberty: An Examination of the Influence of George Mason on the American Bill of Rights, Fairfax County History Commission, 1989.

Siemers, David J., The Antifederalists: Men of Great Faith and Forbearance, Rowman & Littlefield Publishers, 2003.

Slonim, Shlomo, Framers' Construction/Beardian Deconstruction" Essays on the Constitutional Design of 1787, Peter Lanf Publishing, 2001.

Stewart, David, The Summer of 1787: The Men Who Invented the Constitution, Simon & Schuster. 2007.

Storing, Herbert, ed., George Mason and George Washington: What the Anti-Federalists Were For, University of Chicago Press, 1981,

Storing, Herbert J., The Complete Anti-Federalist, University of Chicago Press, 2008.

Tarter, Brent, George Mason and the Conservation of Liberty, The Virginia Magazine of History and Biography, July 1991.

Thompson, C. Bradley, America's Revolutionary Mind: A Moral History of the American Revolution and the Declaration That Defined It, Encounter Books, 2019.

Tiedman, Christopher, The Unwritten Constitution of the United States: A Philosophical Inquiry Into the Fundamentals of American Constutuional Law, G. P. Putnam, 1890.

Timberlake, Richard H., The Central Banking Role of Clearinghouse Associations, Journal of Money, Credit and Banking, 1984.

Vass, Laurie Thomas, After the Collapse of America: The Democratic Republic of America, Gabby Press, 2019.

Vass, Laurie Thomas, America's Final Revolution: Reconstructing Jefferson's American Dream of An Entrepreneurial Capitalist Society, Gabby Press, 2022.

Vile, John, More Than A Plea For a Declaration of Rights, Talbot Publishing, 2019.

White, Richard, "Information, Markets, and Corruption: Transcontinental Railroads in the Gilded Age," The Journal of American History, June 2003.

Wirt, William, Sketches of the Life and Character of Patrick Henry, Andrus Hartford, & Son, 1852.

Wood, Gordon, The Making of the Constitution, Baylor University Press, 1987.

Wood, Gordon, The Radicalism of the American Revolution, Vintage, 1993.

Zuckert, Michael, The Natural Rights Republic: Studies In The Foundation of The American Political Tradition, University of Notre Dame Press, 1996.

www.ingramcontent.com/pod-product-compliance
Lightning Source LLC
LaVergne TN
LVHW020409070526
838199LV00054B/3576